B-29
SUPERFORTRESS

B·29
SUPERFORTRESS

John Pimlott

PRENTICE-HALL, INC.
ENGLEWOOD CLIFFS, NJ
A Bison Book

Library of Congress Cataloging in Publication Data

Pimlott, John.
  B-29 Superfortress.

  (A Reward book)
  "A Bison Book."
  British ed. published under title: B-29 Super Fortress.
  Bibliography: p.
  1. B-29 bomber.   2. Aeronautics, Military—United
States—History.   I. Title.
UG1242.B6P54   1983   940.54'4973   83-4541
ISBN 0-13-056721-3 (pbk.)

10 9 8 7 6 5 4 3 2 1

ISBN 0-13-056721-3 (PBK.)

This book is available at a special discount when ordered in
bulk quantities. Contact Prentice-Hall, Inc., General
Publishing Division, Special Sales, Englewood Cliffs, N.J. 07632.

Prentice-Hall International, Inc., *London*
Prentice-Hall of Australia Pty. Limited, *Sydney*
Prentice-Hall Canada Inc., *Toronto*
Prentice-Hall of India Private Limited, *New Delhi*
Prentice Hall of Japan, Inc., *Tokyo*
Prentice-Hall of Southeast Asia Pte. Ltd., *Singapore*
Whitehall Books Limited, *Wellington, New Zealand*
Editora Prentice-Hall do Brasil Ltda., *Rio de Janeiro*

Page 1: Colonel Paul Tibbetts in the most famous B-29 of them all -
Enola Gay, the first atomic bomber.
Page 2-3: A B-29B in flight (note the absence of ventral turrets).
Page 4-5: A standard B-29 runs up its R-3350 engines.

CONTENTS

INTRODUCTION

At 0816 on 6 August 1945 the Japanese city of Hiroshima ceased to exist. A 9000lb bomb, nicknamed 'Little Boy,' had, in less than a millisecond, produced an explosion equivalent to 20,000 tons of TNT, generating a flash of heat and a blast wave which ignited and then flattened the target area, killing approximately 78,000 people and injuring a further 51,000. It was the first atomic strike, constituting the dawn of a new and terrible era in warfare whereby heavier-than-air machines could literally tear the heart out of an enemy state, destroying with relative ease its capacity and will to wage war. The Hiroshima raid, together with another against Nagasaki three days later, was carried out by an American B-29 'Superfortress' bomber of the 509th Composite Group from Tinian in the Marianas Islands of the Central Pacific. Its actions on that August morning ensured the aircraft type a permanent place in history. The B-29 became an instrument of death of unparalleled proportions, the ultimate equipment in man's constant search for methods of mass destruction.

In truth the B-29 was neither designed nor contemplated specifically for the atomic mission. The aircraft had its origins in the period between the two world wars, when men were recovering from the terrible destruction, both physical and moral, which had characterized the Great War of 1914–18, and were trying desperately to understand how the trends and developments of that conflict might affect the future of war. The most important of these developments was undoubtedly that of air power, for although the conquest of the air dated back to the exploits of Orville and Wilbur Wright on 17 December 1903, it had taken World War I for military principles and roles to become established. During that conflict intrepid pilots of many nations had shown the capabilities of their machines, initially in reconnaissance, then in air-to-air combat and finally, in the spring of 1917, in what became known as strategic bombing. On 13 June and 7 July 1917 German Gotha bombers, operating from bases in occupied Belgium, had flown virtually unopposed over London and killed about 250 civilians through aerial bombardment. Public reaction in the English capital was dramatic: mobs ran riot in the streets, people decided not to turn up for work in the highly-vulnerable munitions factories and the government of David Lloyd George came under tremendous political pressure to organize some sort of air defense.

The government's reaction was typically British, for in the immediate aftermath of the raids a special committee was set up to investigate what had happened and to recommend ways of preventing any repetition. This committee, chaired by the South African soldier and statesman Jan Christiaan Smuts, reported in considerable haste, probably without fully considering the implications of their findings, and made a number of gloomy forecasts. To Smuts the Gotha raids represented a preview of future war, when the bombing of enemy cities would 'become the principal operations of war, to which the older forms of military and naval operations may become secondary and subordinate.' Although he did initiate a

Left: In-flight photo shows the clean aerodynamic lines of a standard B-29.
Above: Surviving B-29 of the 'Confederate Air Force'; marked as 497th BG, 73rd BW.
Far left: The first strategic bomber: a Gotha GVb in 1917.
Left center: Cottages destroyed by a Zeppelin raid, King's Lynn, 1915.
Below left: Searchlights over the Embankment, London, in 1918.
Below: Bomb damage in London: Odhams' printing house, destroyed 28 January 1918.

Above: **Brigadier General 'Billy' Mitchell in the cockpit of a Morse pursuit plane.**

complex air defense system around London which was in fact quite effective by 1918, he went on to recommend that the only real form of defense was the mounting of a strategic counteroffensive against German cities. He had problems in persuading people to accept this theory at first, but after a series of new German raids in early 1918 which included the dropping of one-ton bombs on London, political and military leaders alike decided to take their response to the heart of Germany itself. On 1 April 1918 the Royal Air Force came into existence as an autonomous service, charged solely with the mounting of a strategic bombing campaign against the enemy state.

In the event, the war ended in armistice before this bombing force could really be organized, and although a few raids were carried out against cities such as Mannheim, Frankfurt and Koblenz and plans were well advanced for hitting Berlin in the spring of 1919, strategic bombing as a policy of war was left as little more than a theory, untested and unproven but frighteningly persuasive. From the evidence of the German attacks on London it seemed that bombers could penetrate air-defense systems with impunity, drop their bombs when and where they liked, undermining the morale of the civilian population and destroying the factories upon which the state depended in fighting modern, technological war. The problems encountered by the Germans in sustaining their offensive – problems of navigation, weather and unreliable aircraft – were conveniently ignored, as were the signs of growing air defense capability shown by the anti-aircraft guns and interceptor fighters of Britain in 1918. To many people, Smuts was right. In the event of future war, military and naval campaigns would be relatively unimportant; the decisive operations would be carried out by waves of bombers flying freely over vulnerable heartland targets.

It was not in everyone's interests to believe such stories, and in most of the modern states of the world army and navy leaders fought hard to undermine and discredit the ideas of their air colleagues. In Britain this took the form of attempts, throughout the 1920s and early 1930s, to disband the RAF as a separate service, thereby returning air power back into the hands of the other two arms. In other states, notably America, it was manifested by a conscious policy of preventing autonomy from developing at all. Despite the theories of people such as Giulio Douhet in Italy, Sir Hugh Trenchard in Britain and Brigadier General William ('Billy') Mitchell in America,

by the early 1930s a paradoxical situation had arisen. Few air forces were organized for strategic bombing but the idea itself had both caught and terrified the public imagination. It was not until the 1930s had produced the specter of fascism in Europe, particularly that associated with National Socialism in Germany, that the politicians of the 'Free World' began to stir. To many commentators, they were almost too late.

One of the most vociferous of these commentators was Billy Mitchell, for although he was to die in February 1936, he had laid the groundwork of strategic bombing in America. An air commander with the American Expeditionary Force in France in 1917–18, he had been deeply impressed by the potential of aerial bombardment on the proposed RAF pattern and had returned to the United States intent upon gaining strategic autonomy for what was then a divided air corps, tied inextricably to providing tactical support to land and naval forces. To Mitchell strategic bombing was a natural war policy for the United States; the country was isolated between two immense oceans, making response to any attack upon her interests overseas dependent upon a long and costly process of preparing and dispatching military or naval forces to the scene of action. By comparison aircraft could provide an immediate response, appearing almost instantaneously over the enemy state to threaten or even carry out aerial bombardment. A fleet of bombers was therefore cheaper and more effective than a fleet of vulnerable battleships or a large, slow-moving army.

Mitchell did not succeed in his self-appointed task – he was in fact court-martialled and forced to resign his commission 'for five years' in 1925 after having made a particularly heated public attack upon his superiors – but he did manage to influence enough members of the next generation of American air officers to ensure that his ideas did not die with him. They were tacitly supported by a continuing trend of improvement in aeronautical engineering and aircraft design in America which at least made sure that if Mitchell's theories were ever accepted by the strategists and planners in Washington, the necessary equipment would be available.

Well to the forefront in the field of aerial technology during this period was the Boeing Aircraft Company of Seattle, Washington, which produced a series of innovatory designs for long-range bombers, based in part upon their experience and expertise in the field of commercial airliners. In 1930 Boeing produced what became known as the B-9, the world's first all-metal, twin-engined, monoplane bomber, and when an experimental model was tested by the Army Air Corps (AAC) at Wright Field, Dayton, Ohio, in April 1931 Army planners were sufficiently impressed to order six for further evaluation. With a top speed of 188mph at 6000ft and a bomb-load capacity of 2000lb, the B-9 was the beginning of the development trend which was to produce the B-29 nine years later.

Boeing was not the only company in the arena, and in July 1932 the Glenn L Martin Company of Baltimore, Maryland, improved significantly upon the performance of the B-9. Their B-10 all-metal, twin-engined, monoplane bomber, introducing the innovation of a retractable undercarriage, reached 197mph. Three months later, with new engines fitted, this speed was pushed over the 200mph mark and the Army gained permission to purchase 48 of the type. In 1934 one of Mitchell's most able disciples, Lieutenant Colonel Henry ('Hap') Arnold, led a flight of B-10s nonstop from Juneau, Alaska, to Seattle, illustrating the potential for long-range bombing and national defense which such aircraft possessed. It may be presumed that the lessons were not entirely wasted, for it was about this time that the AAC planners began to put forward specifications for even more modern designs. One of these, issued in 1934, was satisfied by the B-18 from the Douglas Aircraft Company of Santa Monica, California, and 133 examples of this twin-engined monoplane, capable of carrying 4400lb of bombs over 2000 miles at 217mph, were ordered in January 1936.

Meanwhile the Boeing designers had not been idle. In the summer of 1934 they produced an experimental four-engined machine, known as the XB-15, to satisfy a very optimistic Army demand, Project A, for a long-range bomber capable of carrying 2000lb over something like 5000 miles. This attempt to produce an aircraft which would extend the capability of the AAC beyond the realms of national defense into those of strategic bombing proper had disappointing results – the XB-15 was far too heavy for the available engines and only managed 197mph – but Boeing had learned a great deal. They were now well ahead of their rivals in four-engined design and its problems, so when the Army toned down its specifications to the more modest range of 2000 miles, the Company was ready with a design, having already produced a mockup at their own expense. This became the highly successful B-17 'Flying Fortress' and, despite a prototype crash on 30 October 1935, this design was the only truly modern bomber in the AAC inventory when America found herself at war in late 1941. Much of the technological knowledge which was to be devoted to the B-29 design came from the manufacture of this aircraft.

Thus by the mid-1930s the AAC had begun to acquire the equipment necessary for the implementation of Mitchell's ideas, but as yet they lacked the political backing to expand their forces and to plan their future strategy. This gradually developed as events in Europe unfolded toward war, for although many Americans were intent upon a policy of isolation from affairs abroad, certain incidents were beginning to penetrate their protective shell. Many of these involved air power, for while the AAC had been slowly building up its design base, other states, particularly Germany, had been rearming and testing their new equipment in combat. On 26 April 1937 elements of the German Condor Legion, supporting General Franco's forces in the Spanish Civil War, bombed the Basque town of Guernica in a raid which sent shivers of apprehension through the people of Europe. The peripheral shock waves even reached Washington, and when the obvious potential of the Luftwaffe was added to the known successes of Japanese air power over Chinese cities, President Franklin D Roosevelt began to consider the question of American defense. He was particularly concerned about the apparent paralysis of Britain and France in their dealings with an expan-

Above: **Brigadier General William 'Billy' Mitchell.**

sionist Hitler, recognizing that this arose in large measure from the fears of Luftwaffe raids upon their respective cities. Intent upon preventing a similar situation in America, in January 1937 Roosevelt requested an appropriation of $300 million from Congress to enable the AAC to build up its strength, ostensibly as a deterrent. This request was granted on 3 April and the AAC planners were given the green light.

Time was not wasted. Even while Congress was deliberating, Arnold – by now a major general and acting head of the AAC – had consulted the famous airman Charles A Lindbergh about the current state of German aeronautical engineering. Lindbergh, recently returned from a detailed tour of Luftwaffe factories and bases, was convinced that Germany was well ahead of her potential European rivals. He was able to persuade Arnold that the AAC must look very seriously indeed at the future of aerial technology if America was not to be left far behind. As a result Lindbergh was appointed to a special committee, chaired by Brigadier General W G Kilner, which was directed to examine and report on the long-term needs of the AAC. A report was produced in late June 1939 which recommended the immediate initiation of plans to develop several new long-range medium and heavy bombers. Official consideration of these suggestions was hastened considerably by the outbreak of war in Europe on 1 September. On 10 November Arnold felt bold enough to request authority to contract major aircraft companies for studies of a Very Long-Range (VLR) bomber, capable of carrying any future war well beyond the shores of America. Approval was granted on 2 December and AAC engineering officers under Captain Donald L Putt of Material Command at Wright Field began to prepare their official specification. The B-29 was about to be conceived.

Below: **Mitchell (center, with stick) and staff, Koblenz, 1919.**

DEVELOPMENT

The official letter, containing Request for Data R-40B and Specification XC-218, arrived on the desk of Philip G Johnson, President of the Boeing Company, on 5 February 1940. It was an ambitious proposal, calling for a bomber with a range of 5333 miles yet with a bigger bomb load and higher speed than the B-17. Moreover initial designs had to be submitted within thirty days.

Fortunately the Boeing Company was well prepared. After the failure of the XB-15 in 1934 the drawings had not been scrapped but worked upon, at the Company's expense, to produce plans for Model 316. The B-17 had been improved, at least on paper, to become Model 322. Further Company specifications had been produced in 1939 and in December of that year, again at their own expense, a full-scale mockup of Model 341 had been produced, envisaging wing loadings as high as 64lb per sq ft, a twelve-man crew and an ability to carry 2000lb of bombs over distances in excess of 5000 miles. This was remarkably close to Specification XC-218 and the design, slightly reworked, was submitted to the AAC within the set deadline. At the same time, similar designs were produced by the Douglas, Lockheed and Consolidated aircraft companies. As it turned out, all were asked to resubmit in April, after incorporating into their designs such items as leakproof fuel tanks and armor protection, found by the combatants in Europe at the time to be of paramount importance.

The new bids were evaluated in May 1940 by a special AAC Board under Colonel Oliver P Echols of Material Command and two designs were initially favored, those of Lockheed and Boeing, with the latter, now known as Model 345, receiving unofficial preference. It was an impressive design, contemplating a pressurized aircraft (the first of its kind for purely military use) capable of carrying one ton of bombs over the stipulated 5333 miles at a cruising speed of about 290mph. It was to have four engines, a twelve-man crew and a tricycle undercarriage (again, an innovation for a heavy bomber) with double wheels all round. It was to be defended by four retractable turrets, each mounting twin 0.5in machine guns, and a tail turret with twin machine guns and a 20mm cannon. The wing span was to be an awesome 141ft 2in, the length 98ft and the weight 97,700lb. Colonel Echols' Board gave it the AAC designation XB-29.

Below: **B-29As in various stages of production at the Boeing factory in Renton, Washington, 1944.**

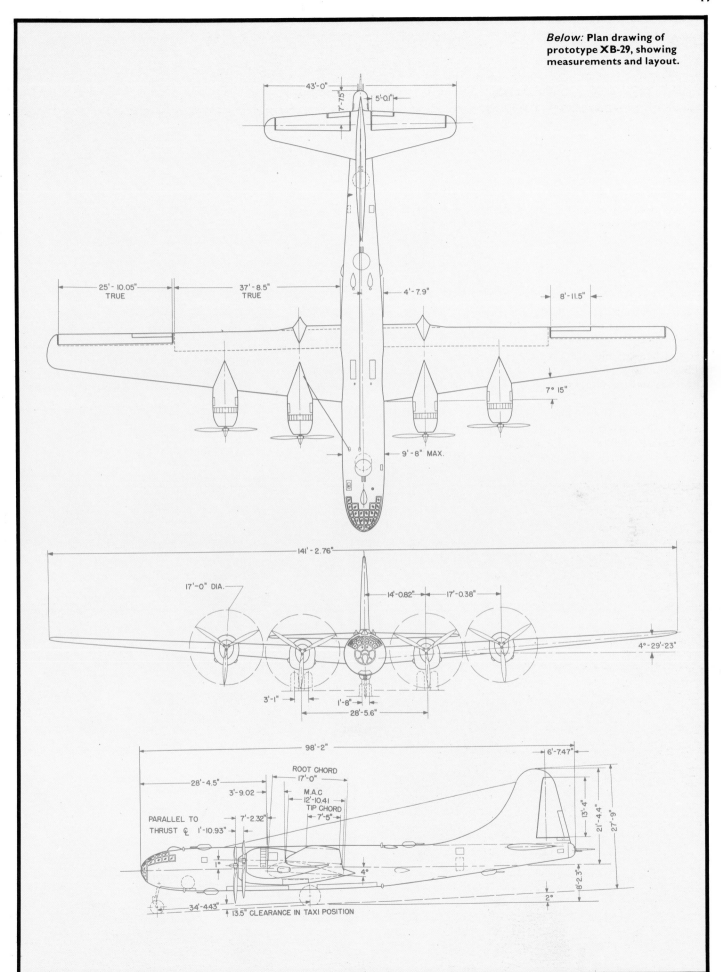

Eddie
ALLEN

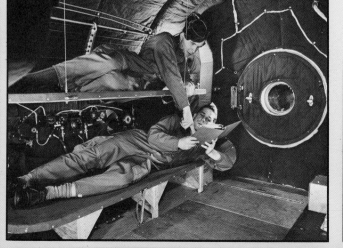

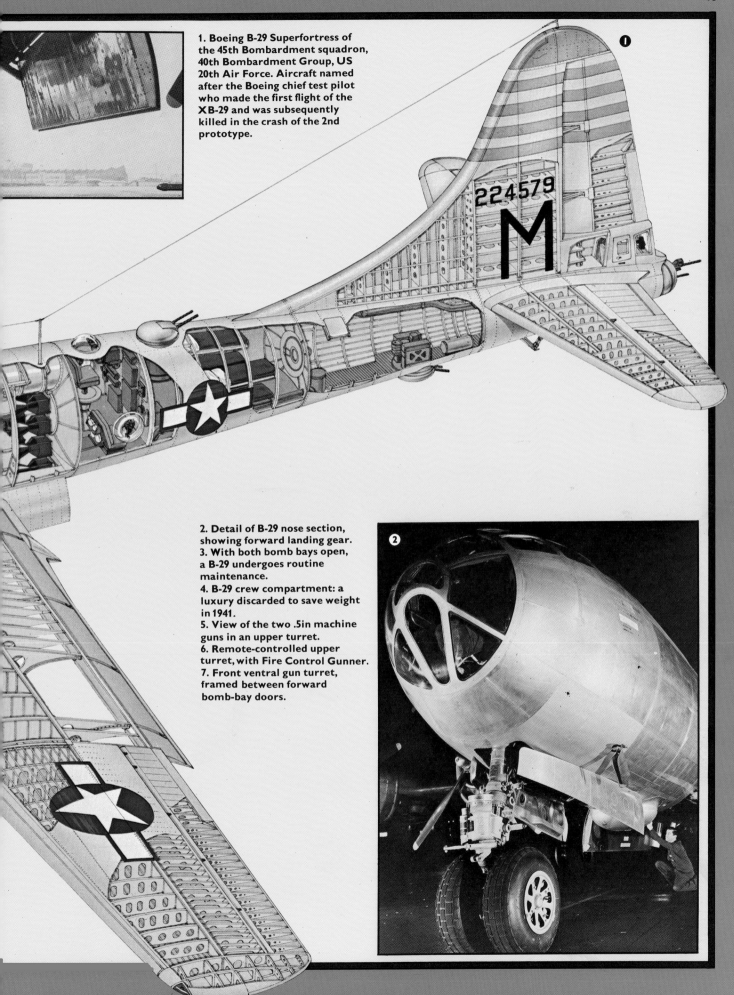

1. Boeing B-29 Superfortress of the 45th Bombardment squadron, 40th Bombardment Group, US 20th Air Force. Aircraft named after the Boeing chief test pilot who made the first flight of the XB-29 and was subsequently killed in the crash of the 2nd prototype.

2. Detail of B-29 nose section, showing forward landing gear.
3. With both bomb bays open, a B-29 undergoes routine maintenance.
4. B-29 crew compartment: a luxury discarded to save weight in 1941.
5. View of the two .5in machine guns in an upper turret.
6. Remote-controlled upper turret, with Fire Control Gunner.
7. Front ventral gun turret, framed between forward bomb-bay doors.

224579 M

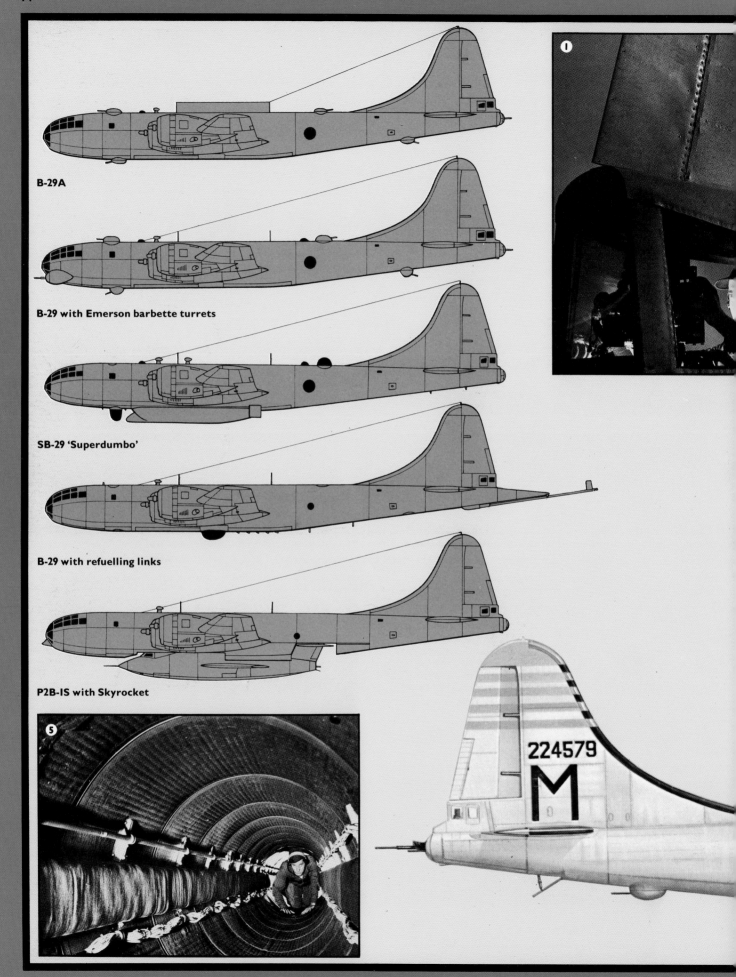

B-29A

B-29 with Emerson barbette turrets

SB-29 'Superdumbo'

B-29 with refuelling links

P2B-IS with Skyrocket

224579

M

1. Tail gunner shows the sighting and firing mechanism for his weapons.
2. Typical tail-gun array – one 20mm cannon and two .5in machine guns.
3. General layout of the gun-control system on a standard B-29.
4. B-29 *Eddie Allen*, 40th BG, 58th BW.
5. Pressurized tunnel linking forward and mid-plane crew areas of a B-29.

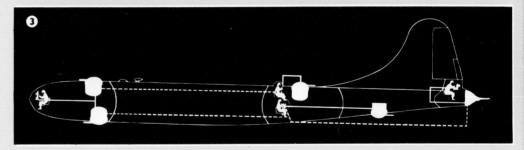

On 4 June 1940 Arnold authorized both Boeing and Lockheed to produce mockups of their designs for wind-tunnel tests and to deliver prototypes to the Wright Field testing center for evaluation. Such was the preparedness of the Boeing Company that it completed preliminary designs by 24 August, enabling Arnold to contract officially for two XB-29 prototypes (at a cost of $3,615,095) on 6 September. Full-scale mockups were ready by late November and when AAC engineering officers visited Seattle they were so impressed that a third prototype was added to the order. By this time Lockheed had decided to withdraw from the competition (their XB-30 never in fact flew), and although the second contract was transferred to Consolidated and the XB-32 – which was eventually to be produced as the B-32 'Dominator' – Boeing were so far advanced that their design was virtually assured of success.

This did not mean that the production of the XB-29 was straightforward: far from it. The design was so advanced and, in some respects, almost revolutionary, that problems were sure to arise. The first of these concerned the wing, for Boeing were, to all intents and purposes, attempting to achieve a technological breakthrough. The difficulty was air resistance, for in an aircraft as heavy as the XB-29 the load borne by each square foot of wing surface was astronomical by contemporary standards. Although it was perfectly feasible that the aircraft, with 1736sq ft of wing area, would fly, its landing speed would be prohibitively high. Boeing designers got around the problem by developing huge flaps, covering 332sq ft of wing area so that, in effect, almost one-sixth of the wings could be lowered to reduce landing speeds. It gave the aircraft a distinctively long, thin wing which, at first glance, looked incapable of supporting the machine in the air and which many airmen distrusted on sight. What they could not see, however, were the immensely strong trusses, constructed in a web-like pattern out of flat pieces of sheet metal, which Boeing engineers had specially developed. The result was a robust aircraft, the clean lines of which were considerably enhanced by the decision to countersink all rivet heads until they lay flush with the aluminum alloy skin surfaces. In the end the XB-29 looked rather like a long, smooth cigar.

Another problem concerned pressurization, for although a cabin supercharger of proven design was available (Boeing had already used it in their commercial Stratoliner of the 1930s), the principle was endangered by the obvious need to open bomb bays during high-altitude flight. Again the designers came up with a solution, this time by producing two areas of pressurization – the extensively glazed control cabin at the front and the gunners' area amidships – connected by a tunnel, big enough at 34in diameter for a man to crawl through, but totally separate from the non-pressurized bomb bays. A third compartment in the tail, unconnected to the others, housed the rear gunner. It was another distinctive feature of the aircraft and rendered its legend even more memorable.

However, not all the problems could be solved at Seattle, for certain areas of design were outside the full control of the Boeing Company. The most important of these concerned the engines, which were chosen by the AAC. They favored the Wright Aeronautical Corporation's R-3350 (the number refers to the total displacement in cubic inches), an eighteen-cylinder air-cooled radial engine, capable of producing 2200bhp at takeoff, and turning a three-bladed 17ft diameter propeller.

Left: **B-29s under inspection at Marietta, Georgia, before delivery to Bombardment Squadrons.**

Unfortunately, although this had been designed and tested in 1937, achieving the desired power through the addition of a pair of General Electric B-11 exhaust-driven turbo-superchargers automatically regulated by a Minneapolis-Honeywell electronic system, the engine had not been put into production. In mid-1940 only one example existed, necessitating a speed of production which was to cause persistent problems.

In addition, as work on the prototypes progressed, the AAC insisted upon a phenomenal number of design changes, totalling nearly 900 between mid-1940 and late 1942, in the light of lessons emerging from the war in Europe. The most significant of these concerned the armament of the XB-29, for although the original retractable turrets supplied by Sperry were satisfactory, in late 1941 the firm of General Electric came up with a revolutionary new design. Centered upon a small computer which could correct automatically for range, altitude, air speed and temperature, it produced a central control mechanism which would enable any gunner (except the man in the tail) to take over more than one of the four 0.5in turrets at one time. Thus a gunner without a target could pass control of his turret over to a colleague who was tracking an enemy aircraft. In addition, as the whole system was remote controlled anyway, it was possible for the gunners (again, with the exception of the man in the tail) to be physically removed from their guns, so escaping the noise and vibrations of combat. The concept was too good to ignore, and Boeing were directed to incorporate it regardless of the time-loss involved. Unfortunately such sophistication required a lot of electrical power, necessitating the addition of a large number of specially-designed generators to the aircraft. This delayed production still further and, rather ominously, increased the weight of the aircraft to 105,000lb, even after such luxuries as auxiliary crew bunks and cabin soundproofing had been dispensed with.

Nevertheless, as early as May 1941, before any of the prototypes had even been test flown, the AAC – soon to be renamed the Army Air Force (AAF) – ordered 250 of what now became the B-29. Boeing immediately expanded its work force, opened a new factory at Wichita, Kansas, and, following an increase in the order to 500 after the Japanese air attack on Pearl Harbor had catapulted America into the war, started to subcontract parts of the production process. The Fisher Division of General Motors was charged with producing all the necessary castings, forgings and stampings and both the Bell Aircraft Corporation and North American Aviation were contracted to produce B-29 subassemblies. Factories at Marietta, Georgia, and Kansas City were constructed to assemble the aircraft in their final form.

All this took place in early 1942 and the B-29 had yet to take to the air. Because of all the problems and delays it was not until early September that the first prototype was finally wheeled out of the factory at Seattle to begin taxi tests. Boeing's chief test pilot, Edmund T ('Eddie') Allen – winner of the 1939 Chanute Award for services to aeronautical sciences – ran the engines up initially on 9 September, and lifted the aircraft off the ground in three short hops of about 15ft altitude six days later. He was not completely satisfied with the engines – according to estimates at the time they could barely last an hour before becoming dangerously overheated – but on 21 September 1942 XB-29 Number One took off on a 75-minute flight. Allen was impressed, as was the AAF project officer, Donald Putt (now a Colonel) when he took it up next day. He scribbled his impressions as he flew, noting that it was 'unbelievable for such a large plane to be so easy on controls . . ., easier to fly than B-17 . . ., faster than any previous heavy bomber . . ., control forces very light . . ., stall characteristics remarkable for heavy plane. . . .' These impressions were reinforced on 2 December when, after eighteen hours flight-testing time had been accrued, the prototype was taken up to 25,000ft for the first time. It was clear that the aircraft had the potential to meet the exacting terms of Specification XC-218.

This was a false dawn, soon to be darkened by persistent examples of engine failure. On 28 December the number one R-3350 of the prototype caught fire, forcing Allen to return prematurely to Boeing Field. Two days later, during the maiden flight of XB-29 Number Two, a similar occurrence led to a suspension of further tests. They were renewed on 18 February 1943, only to end in disaster as a double engine fire in the second prototype led to the death of Allen and the entire test crew. It began to look as if Boeing were suffering from a prototype jinx.

Arnold ordered an immediate investigation into the accident, which soon discovered that the fault lay in the hurried production of the R-3350s – an inevitable by-product of the original choice of engine for which no one could really be held to blame. Nevertheless, with further testing of the XB-29

now virtually stopped, the VLR concept was taking on the appearance of an illusion. Something had to be done very quickly indeed to prevent a cancellation of the entire project and with it an end to the strategic dreams of the AAF. Arnold was well aware of this and in mid-April 1943 he set up what was known as the 'B-29 Special Project' under the command of Brigadier General Kenneth B Wolfe. He was told to take charge of the entire B-29 program, including production, flight testing and crew training, with a view to combat commitment by the end of the year. It was a tall order, nearly cut short on 29 May when the third XB-29 prototype was saved from disaster by the opportune discovery, just before takeoff, that the aerilon cables had been connected the wrong way round. However, the wider events of the war, particularly in the Pacific, were demanding the commitment of ever-larger forces. The role to be played by the B-29 was under intense discussion even while the prototypes were being tested.

Above right: **B-29s take shape in the huge, purpose-built hangar at Wichita, Kansas.**
Below: **Early production B-29 takes off from Boeing Field, Wichita, the new plant expanded for B-29 production.**

PREPARING FOR COM

President Roosevelt had long been interested in the possibility of bombing Japan. Before Pearl Harbor he had often discussed with his more immediate advisers plans for providing long-range bombers for the Chinese leader Chiang Kai-shek so that he could retaliate for the air attacks which had been mounted against his cities since the beginning of the Sino–Japanese war in 1937. One of these proposals had almost come to fruition in December 1940 when, on the advice of the Secretary of State Cordell Hull and Secretary of the Treasury Henry Morgenthau, Roosevelt had actually promised to transfer some of the new B-17s to Chinese hands on the express understanding that they would be used against Japanese cities. It was only after General George Marshall, Chief of Staff to the Army, had pointed out that there were barely enough B-17s for American needs that the idea was dropped. Chiang Kai-

shek had to be satisfied with 100 fighter planes instead, but the incident showed how Roosevelt's mind was working. It was therefore no surprise that he returned to the theme of bombing Japan almost immediately after Pearl Harbor.

Unfortunately, despite the growing interest in Mitchell's ideas and the development of the B-17, the AAF – for too long the Cinderella of the services – was in no position to mount an immediate campaign. In accordance with the strategic principles laid down at the Anglo–American Arcadia Conference in Washington (22 December 1941 – 14 January 1942), the emphasis was to be placed upon defeating the Axis powers in Europe first, after which the Allies would be able to devote their full strength against Japan. Given the political realities of the time, particularly the fact that Germany was threatening the territorial integrity of the Allied homelands far more than

AT

Below: Standard B-29 on crew-familiarization flight, 1944.

Japan was, this was probably quite sensible. However it did mean that the products of American war industry were channelled across the Atlantic rather than the Pacific. Thus, for example, the majority of B-17s produced in 1942 were sent to build up the 8th Army Air Force stationed in England, and few found their way to the Pacific theater.

Even if large numbers of B-17s had been available, they could hardly have achieved a great deal against the Japanese homeland for the simple reason of geography. During the extraordinary run of Japanese successes between December 1941 and June 1942 all the Pacific bases capable of sustaining bomber formations within range of Japan – the Philippines, Wake, Guam, the Dutch East Indies – had all been lost by the Allies, leaving the Americans with very few options indeed if Roosevelt's demands for action were to be met. One possi-

bility was explored by Colonel James H Doolittle on 18 April 1942 when he led a surprise raid on Tokyo by specially-modified B-25 carrier-borne bombers, but the enterprise was extremely costly. Not only were all sixteen of the bombers lost, but the people of China, to whom the surviving crews turned for aid after baling out of their stricken craft, suffered terribly when the Japanese mounted a land offensive to capture all territory within flying range of their home islands.

Doolittle's raid did boost Allied morale at a difficult time in the war, however, and probably made Roosevelt all the more determined to initiate a more permanent bombing campaign, resurrecting his former ideas about basing the aircraft in China. He began by authorizing an airlift of supplies from India, over the Hump of the Himalayas, to bolster Chiang Kai-shek's forces. By January 1943, at the Casablanca Conference of Allied leaders, he was openly discussing sending '200 to 300 planes' to China, including heavy bombers. It was envisaged that the latter aircraft, which, given the state of development of the B-29 at the time, must have been B-17s or B-24 Liberators, would be based in eastern India, merely using Chinese bases to refuel on their long haul to Japan. However problems of supply – sufficient transport aircraft were just not available to support a bombing campaign in such adverse geographical conditions – coupled with the fact that neither the B-17 nor the B-24 really had the ranges to make the journeys involved, prevented any further action being taken. Moreover, with the gradual build-up of air operations against Germany and the plans for an invasion of occupied Europe taking strategic precedence, the resources, even of a mobilized America, could not satisfy the demands of a two-front war in this way.

The picture began to change in August 1943 when, at the Quadrant Conference at Quebec, Arnold submitted an 'Air Plan for the defeat of Japan.' This document contained the first reference in strategic policy to the B-29. Up to that time a rather vague proposal for committing the new bombers to Europe had existed – it was envisaged that twelve groups would be stationed in Northern Ireland and twelve near Cairo, Egypt – but Arnold's plan was much more specific. He proposed the deployment of the 58th Bombardment Wing (Very Heavy), newly activated under Wolfe's command and organized to contain four groups of B-29s, to the China, Burma, India (CBI) theater by the end of the year. Following Mitchell's beliefs on strategic bombing almost to the letter, Arnold expressed confidence that once the B-29 was available in sufficient numbers (he envisaged a total deployment of 780 in the CBI), the bombers could bring Japan to her knees in something like six months through the destruction of her war industries. They were to be stationed permanently in China, possibly around Chengtu in the south-center of the country, with supplies of fuel, bombs and spares being flown in from eastern India. Full-scale operations, involving the full total of B-29s, would probably not begin much before October 1944, but this could mean that Japan would be defeated, without the need for a costly seaborne invasion, by mid-1945, a date

already projected by the Combined Chiefs of Staff as the end of the war.

Roosevelt was delighted with the concept and followed it up, despite the fact that both the Joint Plans Committee and the Joint Logistics Committee rejected Arnold's plan as strategically unfeasible. He passed the proposal on to Lieutenant General Joseph W ('Vinegar Joe') Stilwell, Chiang Kai-shek's acerbic American Chief of Staff, for evaluation, and was even more delighted when he suggested a return to the President's original plan of eight months earlier. Instead of basing the B-29s in China, Stilwell proposed that they should be maintained in eastern India, merely staging through Chengtu in the process or aftermath of the raids. This had obvious advantages. The raids could begin at the earliest possible date as a complex base facility would not need to be constructed in China and the airfields in India would not be particularly vulnerable to a surprise Japanese land offensive. Also the thorny problem of supply would be simplified, especially if the B-29s themselves could be used to carry fuel, bombs and spares to build up the dumps at Chengtu. The Joint Chiefs of Staff were still not completely convinced, but Roosevelt soon made sure that they had no choice in the matter. On 10 November 1943 he sought, and gained, the co-operation of the British in the provision of bases around Calcutta and persuaded Chiang Kai-shek to begin the construction, with American engineering help, of five new airfields around Chengtu. The B-29 appeared at last to have a strategic role.

However, things rarely go smoothly in wartime and this was no exception. As early as October 1943 Arnold had become concerned about the speed with which the President was preparing his strategy, particularly as he was frequently discussing the first raids being mounted on 1 January 1944. Arnold was forced to inform him that B-29 deployment could not

Right: **B-29 shows its lines and the size of its bomb bays, 1943.**
Far right: **Lt Gen James Doolittle (standing, left) with Vice-Admiral Marc A Mitscher and B-25 crews on board USS *Hornet*, prior to the Tokyo Raid of April 1942.**
Below right: **B-29 over the farmlands of Kansas (note four-gun array in forward dorsal turret and lack of tail cannon: signs of active service).**

Below: **Roosevelt (second from left, seated) and Churchill (right, seated) with advisers, Quebec, August 1943.**

Below: **Roosevelt and Churchill brief war correspondents and service officers, Casablanca, January 1943.**

Below: Four views of Wichita-built B-29, serial number 293869, as it is prepared for squadron delivery.

really begin much before March or April of that year, with the campaign itself commencing on 1 May at the earliest. Roosevelt was bitterly disappointed, chiefly because such delays could well be seen as breaking promises made to China, but he could do little about it. The enormously complex job of preparing the new bombers for combat could simply not be rushed, even under the pressures of war.

First of all, an entirely new command structure had to be set up to ensure that the program of crew training was carried out and that the bombers, once deployed, were capable of performing their strategic task. Arnold began the process in late November 1943, moving Wolfe yet again, this time to the command of a new formation, XX Bomber Command, which would take responsibility for mounting the campaign. The Command was assigned two Bombardment Wings, each of four groups of B-29s – the 58th, the command of which was now transferred from Wolfe to his erstwhile deputy, Colonel Leonard ('Jake') Harmon, and the 73rd, newly-activated under Colonel Thomas H Chapman. Headquarters were set up conveniently close to the B-29 factory at Wichita and responsibility for crew training delegated to Colonel La Verne G ('Blondie') Saunders of the Second Army Air Force. He moved into four airfields in Kansas – Smoky Hill, Pratt, Great Bend and Walker – and began his onerous task.

The crew training program was one of the most complicated aspects of the B-29 story. By late 1943 the size of a typical crew had been settled as eleven, the original Boeing specification of twelve having been reduced by the introduction of the General Electric gun system, which dispensed with the services of one turret gunner. Five members of each crew were officers (the aircraft commander, pilot, bombardier, navigator and flight engineer – although the last-named post did become an enlisted man's responsibility as the war progressed), and six were enlisted men (the radio operator, radar operator, Central Fire Control gunner, left gunner, right gunner and tailgunner), and all required some degree of specialist training. It usually took something like 27

weeks to produce a fully-fledged pilot, fifteen to train a navigator and twelve to produce a competent gunner, and all this had to take place before the men could be brought together and trained specifically for the B-29. Even using the revised deployment schedule put forward by Arnold there was not enough time available to start from scratch, so volunteers were called for among B-24 crews recently returned to America from operations in Europe and North Africa. Even then the problems were by no means solved. The B-29 was a complex piece of machinery, bigger and faster than the B-24 and with more sophisticated equipment on board, necessitating a fairly lengthy process of crew integration before combat deployment could begin. The whole affair was not helped by a unique policy decision to provide each B-29 with two crews, presumably in deference to the enormous distances which would have to be flown once the campaign began.

Saunders thus faced a tremendous task in late 1943, and it is to his credit that enough crews were available when the 58th Bombardment Wing left America for the CBI a few months later. There can be no doubt that the training was of a sketchy nature, partly because of the very tight time schedules involved, but also because of a chronic shortage of B-29s throughout the training period. Crews slowly began to arrive at the Kansas bases in November 1943, fully expecting to be introduced immediately to the new bomber that they had heard so much about. They were invariably disappointed – in fact some of the gunners did not even see a B-29 until early 1944 – and had to be satisfied instead with simulated training on rather tired B-17s. This did at least enable a degree of crew integration to take place – the aircraft commanders, pilots and flight engineers were usually trained for five weeks as separate teams to ensure that they worked together during the complicated and dangerous period of takeoff – but by the end of December a mere 67 pilots had managed to fly a B-29, and very few crews had even been brought together as a complete team. Even those who had were restricted in their training, for the B-17s that were used for formation-flying practice

Right: **The Tokyo Raid of 18 April 1942: one of Doolittle's modified B-25s takes off from USS *Hornet*.**
Below: **B-29B, used for training commanders, pilots and flight engineers, 1944.**

Above: Lt Gen Joseph ('Vinegar Joe') Stilwell, Burma, 1943.
Above left: Stilwell (center) at a planning conference, 1944.
Left: Navigator briefs commander and pilot prior to takeoff on training flight.

Above: Head-on view of production B-29 shows length of wing and tricycle undercarriage (B-17s and B-29s in background).

could barely reach 20,000ft altitude, 8000ft below that envisaged as the operating height of the B-29. The whole production program for the aircraft appeared to have become bogged down.

The main reason for this sorry state of affairs is fairly easy to isolate in retrospect, for Boeing was being asked to produce an almost revolutionary aircraft in an impossibly short time, and their job was not made any easier by the constant call for modifications as the lessons of air combat, particularly in Europe, were assessed. Thus although a total of 97 B-29s had been produced by mid-January 1944, only sixteen were flyable and none had been issued to the 58th Bombardment Wing. They were all in AAF modification centers, chiefly at Marietta, Georgia, undergoing a series of improvements and changes which sometimes took sixty days to complete.

The most important, if not the most time consuming, of these modifications concerned the engines. In the aftermath of the prototype crash in February 1943, the R-3350 had been further developed and improved by the Wright engineers, but problems remained. Some of these were solved by the replacement of the original R-3350-13 packs on the prototypes with R-3350-21 models on the early production aircraft, and this had at least reduced the risk of engine fires spreading to the highly-inflammable aluminum-covered wings. Accidents continued at an alarming rate – between February 1943 and September 1944 something like nineteen B-29s are known to have been lost to engine fires – and yet another R-3350 model, the 23, was developed. Unfortunately these were not ready to be fitted to the aircraft as they came off the production line at Wichita, so they had to be added at the modification centers. At the same time the three-bladed propellers of the XB-29s were replaced by four-bladed ones of 16ft 7in diameter. These were Hamilton Standard Hydromatic propellers, with constant-speed governors and hydraulic operation for pitch control and feathering. They represented an improvement in design, but, of course, took time to provide and fit.

Meanwhile, AAF engineers had to check out the condition of the B-29s to make them combat-ready. They were helped by civilian specialists in certain key areas, notably the General Electric gun system. The comments of one of these men, Philip J Klass, illustrates the immense nature of their task:

The condition of the General Electric system was pretty horrible, and I assume that was true for many others. Wires interconnecting aircraft cables made by newly-trained workers sometimes ran to the wrong pins on connectors. Whoever stripped the insulation off sometimes nicked four or five of the seven strands of wire, and left the connection hanging by only a couple. There were blobs of solder shorting out adjacent pins or sockets in the connectors. We did the best we could to assure that the turret system was operable, but we lacked the time to inspect every wire and every connector, and we could only hope they would hang together. (Quoted by David D Anderton, *B-29 Superfortress at War* Ian Allen, 1978.)

Similar problems were experienced with the radar systems, for the AN/APQ-13 bombing-navigational aid, based upon the British-designed H2S system which provided a blurred but useful radar map of the ground as the aircraft flew over, was a complex piece of kit. The radome, containing a 30in radar antenna, was situated between the two bomb bays on the early B-29s and was particularly vulnerable to dirt and general misuse, so had to be carefully checked. Finally certain combat modifications were added to the list, including the addition of extra fuel tanks for the journey out to India and, as supply problems loomed nearer, special dollies and mounts in the bomb bays so that each B-29 could take a spare engine with it. It was all a lengthy business and it soon began to look as if Arnold's revised promise of 150 bombers in the CBI by mid-April 1944 was not going to be realized.

Faced with this possibility, Arnold made a personal visit to Marietta in mid-February, only to be assured that all would be ready by 10 March when deployment could begin. He planned accordingly and it was not until he and one of his assistants, Major General B E Meyer, arrived at Salina on 9 March to supervise the departure of the B-29s that the full extent of the delays became apparent. The modification program was in complete chaos, with not one of the bombers fully combat-ready or even likely to be so in the immediate future. Appalled at the lack of organization and efficiency, Arnold directed Meyer to take charge, demanding a full report on the state of readiness of every B-29 by the following morning. The resultant burst of frenetic activity – known to those involved as the 'Battle of Kansas' or 'Kansas Blitz' – was remarkable in its achievements. Beginning in mid-March as many technicians and specialists as possible were drafted into the modification centers to work flat out to satisfy the delivery deadline of mid-April. Work went on round-the-clock, often in extremely adverse weather conditions, but the first B-29 was ready by

the end of the month. Others quickly followed, until 150 of them had been handed over to the XX Bomber Command by 15 April.

As soon as the aircraft were received, Wolfe assigned them to squadrons within the 58th Bombardment Wing (the 73rd had not been detailed for the CBI until later in 1944), and they took off for India. It was an enormous journey, covering some 11,530 miles and involving stops at Marrakech, Cairo, Karachi and Calcutta. One B-29 even flew to England first in an attempt to confuse Axis intelligence about the actual theater of operations. The speed of modification and preparation soon began to tell and a number of accidents occurred. These culminated in the week 15–22 April, when a total of five B-29s crashed near Karachi, all from overheated engines. The bombers were immediately grounded while an investigation was mounted.

The results – basically that the R-3350s had not been designed to operate in ground temperatures in excess of 115 degrees Fahrenheit – were wired back to America and the Wright engineers yet again tried to sort out the problems. They concluded that the fault lay in the exhaust valves on the rear row of cylinders which were literally melting under pressure, and to correct it they designed new engine baffles to direct a blast of cooling air onto the stricken area. They also improved the flow of oil to the rear cylinders by installing crossover tubes from the intake to the exhaust port of the five top cylinders on both the front and rear rows. It was a patch-up job, but it did seem to work. B-29 flights were resumed and by 8 May 1944, only just outside the schedule originally put forward by Arnold the previous October, 148 of the bombers had reached Marrakech, with 130 of them actually on their airfields in India. It had been a long and difficult road, but the B-29 was about to enter the war. It was probably fortunate that the commanders and crews of the 58th Bombardment Wing could not see into the future, for their problems were only just beginning.

Below: **B-29 radar operator prepares his AN/APQ-13 bombing-navigational receiver equipment.**

Below: **The worker adjusting the rudder acts as a useful yardstick for the height of a B-29 tail fin.**

THE RAIDS FROM CHI

As the B-29s arrived in eastern India the four Bombardment Groups of the 58th Bombardment Wing were assigned their base locations. The headquarters of the 58th BW, together with the four Bombardment Squadrons of the 40th BG (the 25th, 44th, 45th and 395th) were allocated an airfield at Chakulia, the 444th BG (676th, 677th, 678th and 679th BS) went to Charra; the 462nd BG (768th, 769th, 770th and 771st BS) to Piardoba; and the 468th BG (792nd, 793rd, 794th and 795th BS) to Kharagpur, the latter having already been chosen by Wolfe as the headquarters of XX Bomber Command as a whole. All of these bases, lying to the west of Calcutta, had originally been established in 1942–43 for B-24 Liberators, but engineering difficulties had delayed their being fully prepared for the B-29s, so conditions were poor. The runways were still in the process of being lengthened (from 6000 to 7200ft), and although this did not prevent the movement of the big bombers, it did curtail fully-loaded takeoffs and so impose delays. In fact the 444th BG had only been assigned Charra base as a temporary expedient, for their permanent field at Dudhkundi was not prepared at all. They did not make the move until late May, after which Charra became a transport base for the C-87s and C-46s which formed part of XX Bomber Command's transport fleet.

A similar picture emerged when Wolfe and Saunders (who had taken over command of the 58th BW from Harmon before deployment from America began) flew over the Hump in a pair of B-29s on 24 April to inspect the forward bases around Chengtu. These too were not fully prepared, for although construction work had begun at four sites in the area – Kwanghan, Kuinglai, Hsinching and Pengshan – as early as November 1943, progress had been slow in such remote locations. In the event, the runways and base facilities were literally built by hand, with local Chinese farmers providing the labor. A local village quota of work had been imposed – it was set at fifty workers per 100 households – and by January 1944 some 200,000 people had contributed to the program. They achieved a great deal, supervised and aided by American military construction teams specially flown in, and by 1 May all four bases could just about be used by the B-29s but, once again, conditions were far from ideal. Still, by early May there was cause for some satisfaction. Against tremendous odds 148 B-29s had arrived in the CBI and rudimentary bases were available. It showed what could be achieved under the pressures of war.

It was those same pressures which imposed impossible strains upon the entire project, as Wolfe was soon to discover.

A

Above: Heavy equipment, needed to level the runways around Chengtu, is brought in by air in pieces to be reassembled on the ground.
Below: Chinese laborers survey one of the first B-29s to reach Chengtu – *Eileen* of 444th BG, 58th BW.

He was now part of a command structure which afforded to the AAF an unprecedented degree of operational freedom, equivalent in effect to the air force autonomy so eagerly sought by Mitchell in the 1920s. This had come about as a direct result of the B-29 program, for as word of the new bomber and its capabilities spread, every theater and air force commander in the Far East requested control of its operations. In January 1944, when deployment to the CBI was obvious, Major General Claire L Chennault, commanding 14th USAAF in China, even wrote to Roosevelt with his plea, seeing in the B-29 an answer to his problem of containing and then destroying Japanese air power in his theater. He was backed up by Joseph Stilwell who, although envisaging the B-29s being used primarily against ground rather than air targets, insisted that according to precedent, all air units should be controlled by the senior commander on the spot. Similar requests followed from Admiral Chester Nimitz in the Central Pacific, General Douglas MacArthur in the Southwest Pacific

and even Lord Louis Mountbatten, British Commander in Chief of South-East Asia Command (SEAC). It began to look as if the potential of the new bombers was never going to be realized as they would not be able to escape a plethora of conflicting tactical demands.

Arnold, realizing the dangers, had approached the problem with skill, taking as his yardstick the fact that naval forces did not suffer from the same demands, being controlled from Washington by Admiral Ernest King, a member of the Joint Chiefs of Staff. They were regarded as global forces, affecting all theaters as a whole rather than each individually, and this was the precedent which Arnold used when requesting B-29 autonomy. Armed with support from King, he approached the President, and on 4 April 1944 he authorized the establishment of a special strategic command to be known as 20th Air Force. Commanded by Arnold at JCS level, it was given a specific objective which could have been penned by Mitchell himself. Under the operational codename 'Matterhorn,' the B-29s were to begin 'the earliest possible progressive destruction and dislocation of the Japanese military, industrial and economic systems and to undermine the morale of the Japanese people to a point where their capacity for war is decisively defeated.' Furthermore, it was laid down that the bombers were to be used by no one but Arnold. It was argued that he alone enjoyed the information and expertise needed to appreciate their global nature. He could assign the B-29s to local commanders in a tactical emergency, but at all times the operations were strictly under his control.

This was an extremely significant step for the AAF, pointing the way to an autonomous future, but it did impose tremendous pressure upon the B-29 commanders in the CBI. For once the principle of a strategic role had been established, it was imperative that concrete results should be provided as soon as possible. This meant not only that operations had to begin immediately, but also that they should be seen to succeed. Wolfe suddenly found himself in a very difficult position, under pressure from Arnold to begin the bombing of Japan but faced with an ever-growing mountain of problems in the field.

The most important of these was the persistent one of supply. From the beginning it had been specified that XX BC would be virtually self-sufficient within the CBI, providing its own transport facilities without imposing upon those of other forces in the area. This proved impossible in practice, as the

Above: A manually-operated water pump emphasizes the enormous difficulties of base construction in China.

Above: A Rajputana Rifles soldier guards newly-arrived B-29s in eastern India.
Left: Gangs of Chinese laborers - provided by quota from surrounding villages - prepare one of the Chengtu bases.
Below: B-29s arrive at one of the bases in eastern India; the runway is still being lengthened.

logistics administrators in the theater were quick to discover. Even before the 58th BW arrived in India, the preparation of air bases and build up of stocks had required the provision of 20,000 troop places and 200,000 tons of dry cargo space in a supply system which was already under considerable pressure. The CBI at the best of times did not enjoy priority of shipping or stores, coming a very poor third behind Europe and the Pacific, and an extra burden like the bombing campaign nearly caused it to collapse. Special priorities had to be established in February 1944, but even then a significant proportion of equipment had to be 'borrowed' from the British or diverted from airfields in Assam or the highly important Ledo Road project. Understandably, a number of local commanders began to voice their misgivings.

Nor did the situation improve once the 58th BW arrived, for although they were accompanied by their own fleet of transport aircraft, including a number of converted B-24s (known in their new role as C-87s), it soon became apparent that these were insufficient for the build up of supplies around Chengtu. If the bases in China were to be used at all, they had to contain vast quantities of fuel, bombs and spares, all of which had to be flown in first from eastern India. Some transports were diverted from Air Transport Command in the CBI to help out – a decision which did nothing to quieten complaints from local commanders – but the process was lengthy. In the end the B-29s performed the bulk of the operation, particularly in the transportation of fuel. Following an idea originally mooted in Washington by the Matterhorn planners, selected numbers of bombers were stripped of their armaments systems (except for the guns in the tail) and given as many auxiliary fuel tanks as possible, tied into a special fuel

Below: **Lt Gen Henry H Arnold (left) inspects P-40 Flying Tigers pursuit planes with Brig Gen Claire L Chennault, China, 1943.**

design which incorporated an off-loading manifold. These aircraft could lift seven tons of high-octane at a time, but it was not particularly cost effective. Even on a good day, it took two gallons of fuel burned by the delivery aircraft to transport one gallon to Chengtu. On a bad day, with head winds and diversions to avoid bad weather over the Himalayas, this could rise to twelve gallons for every one delivered.

The results were depressing. Wolfe had been ordered by Arnold to mount the first B-29 operation against Japan on or before 1 May, but as the transport fleet had only managed to deliver 1400 tons of supplies to Chengtu by then, further delays were inevitable. The situation was hindered even more by the launching of the Japanese 'Ichi Go' offensive in central China, which took place on 19 April. The Japanese plan was to attack Honan and then strike south and west toward Changsha and a series of 14th USAAF bases around Kweilin and Liuchow which they imagined were going to be used by the B-29s. Indeed some thought had been devoted to this idea by the American commanders, but it was dropped when the vulnerability of the eastern bases was realized. One big disadvantage of Chengtu was that it was too far west, necessitating long overflights of Japanese-occupied territory in China before the Japanese home islands could be attacked, and even then only bringing the southern island of Kyushu within B-29 range. Kweilin and Liuchow did in fact fall to the Japanese in November 1944, but the real disruption to the B-29s was the problem of supply. As the Japanese offensive gathered pace in late April and early May, Stilwell withdrew the Air Transport Command contingent from Wolfe's operations, slowing the build up at Chengtu still further.

Meanwhile, Arnold was pressing for action of some description and, despite the paucity of supplies, Wolfe felt obliged to act. The Hump route was in fact so dangerous and difficult that each time a B-29 flew the 1000 miles involved it counted as a combat mission (and was usually signified as such by the painting of a camel on the aircraft nose). After tremendous transport efforts sufficient stocks were built up to order a 'shakedown' raid. This took place on 5 June and the target was the Makasan railroad yard at Bangkok, Thailand. The raid was a disaster. Some 98 B-29s took off from eastern India on what was a 2000-mile round trip, but fourteen aborted before reaching the target, mostly because of engine problems. The aircraft were supposed to fly in four-plane diamond formations, but this was never fully achieved. The target was overcast, necessitating bombing by radar. The formations became so confused that aircraft dropped their loads at altitudes anywhere between 17–27,000ft instead of the envisaged 22–25,000ft. A mere eighteen bombs landed in the target area; five B-29s crashed on landing and a further 42 were forced to put down at bases which were not their own as fuel ran out. It was an extremely inauspicious start to a campaign which was supposed to be decisive.

The pressure on Wolfe did not ease, for Arnold was now insisting upon a raid against Japan, the first since Doolittle's attack over two years previously. After more tremendous efforts, enough supplies were stockpiled to enable 68 B-29s to take off on 14 June against the Imperial Iron and Steel Works at Yawata, on the island of Kyushu. Some 47 of the bombers made it to the target, this time arriving during the hours of darkness, but results were if anything even worse. Only one hit was recorded and that was three-quarters of a mile from

Left: Chennault (right) receives a decoration from Chiang Kai-shek.
Right: Chennault (left) with Maj Gen A C Wedemeyer, C in C China Theater, 1944.
Below: B-29s of 468th BG, 58th BW, attack targets near Rangoon.

the aiming point. In addition a further six B-29s were destroyed in accidents and one – the first of many – went down to enemy fire. The XX BC was quite clearly failing to carry out its strategic role.

Nevertheless this did not prevent the Yawata raid being hailed as almost a victory in the United States, and the resultant glare of publicity merely heightened Arnold's desire for more attacks. On 16 June he ordered Wolfe to send the B-29s 'the length and breadth of the Japanese Empire.' With fuel stocks at Chengtu down to less than 5000 gallons this was clearly impossible since it took 8800 gallons to send just one B-29 against Japan. Wolfe had no hesitation in saying so, an action which led to his recall to Washington on 4 July. He was promoted and reassigned, leaving Saunders in temporary command in the CBI.

While awaiting Wolfe's replacement, Saunders continued the bombing operations as and when he could. On 7 July eighteen B-29s paid a return visit to Kyushu, dropping bombs (fairly ineffectively) on targets at Sasebo, Nagasaki, Omura and Yawata. Two days later 72 of the bombers flew against a steel-making complex at Anshan in Manchuria. Four aircraft were lost on the latter raid and results were poor, affecting less than eight percent of the industrial facility. This picture was repeated on the night of 10–11 August when 56 B-29s, staging through British air bases at Ceylon, hit oil storage tanks at Palembang in Borneo. It was almost as if the campaign was drifting from target to target, with no real purpose or long-term aim. This undoubtedly reflected the command vacuum at Kharagpur, but the fact that some of the raids took place in the day while others were at night implied a lack of operational control and combat technique. To put it bluntly, Matterhorn had stagnated.

All this changed on 29 August when Wolfe's replacement, Major General Curtis E LeMay, arrived in the CBI. A forceful personality and superb air leader, LeMay had received praise (and accelerated promotion) for his handling of the 3rd Bombardment Division of the 8th AAF in Europe, and Arnold was confident that he could inject some life into XX BC. He was not to be disappointed, for although the first B-29 raid experienced by LeMay against Anshan on 8 September was by far the most successful to date, with relatively few abortions and a reasonable bombing pattern, he was not slow to impose a number of sweeping changes upon the Command. In the sphere of operational technique, he began by replacing the four-plane diamond formation by one of twelve aircraft grouped in a defensive box along the lines used by the B-17s in Europe. This he regarded as imperative if his second reform was to stand any chance of success, for he now insisted upon daylight, precision attacks at all times, again on the European pattern, to make sure that tactical expertise could be gained. In order to achieve the best results from such tactics he also introduced the concept of lead crews who would bear responsibility for finding and marking the target area, an idea which RAF Bomber Command, with its Pathfinder Squadrons, had found exceptionally useful over Germany. Finally, having witnessed some of the problems facing the B-29 crews over Anshan, LeMay ordered that in future both the bombardier and radar operator should control the bombing run, so that whoever had sight of the target at the critical moment could release the bombs. It was hoped that this would save confusion should the target be covered in patchy cloud or haze, conditions which were common in the Far East.

Complementary to these operational changes was a radical reorganization of the 58th BW, designed to simplify and rationalize its basic structure. The prevailing system of four Bombardment Groups, each of four squadrons with seven

B-29s per squadron, was scrapped and the junior squadron from each group (the 395th, 679th, 771st and 795th BS) was disbanded. This left each group with three squadrons of ten B-29s each, an organization which, it was argued, would be easier to administer and control.

It obviously took time for these changes to have any effect – another raid against Anshan on 26 September failed to prove much one way or another – but very gradually things began to improve. On 25 October, for example, an attack upon the Omura aircraft factory on Kyushu showed signs of success, particularly in the use of a two-to-one mixture of high explosive and incendiary bombs. This was repeated on 11 November when the Chinese city of Nanking, occupied by the Japanese since 1937, suffered substantial damage. Practical problems of supply and aircraft accidents were still conspiring to prevent the concentration of force and effort which strategic bombing required to be effective, and these were joined by the new menace of growing Japanese resistance. On 21 November Omura was revisited and the B-29s met solid opposition from interceptor fighters and light bombers (the latter being used to drop phosphorous explosives into the B-29 formations) and six of the Superfortresses failed to return. A similar loss rate occurred on 7 December over the Manchurian Aircraft Company plant at Mukden. In fact B-29 losses were soon reaching prohibitively high levels. When losses from all causes – accident, enemy interception and, in September particularly, Japanese air raids on the Chengtu bases –

were added together at the end of 1944, they came to the sobering total of 147. In other words, the equivalent of the entire B-29 strength in the CBI on 1 May had been wiped out in something like eight months.

It was apparent that despite LeMay's leadership the raids were too expensive and would have to be stopped. A pointer to the future was perhaps provided on the 18 December when 94 B-29s, operating in a tactical emergency as the Japanese approached Kunming, hit the enemy supply base at Hankow in a low-level fire raid, but by then it was too late. Soon after this attack a decision was made by the JCS to phase out the Chengtu operations and instead to concentrate all the B-29s on the newly-captured Marianas Islands in the central Pacific.

The last raid out of China was flown on 15 January 1945, but that too was tactical in concept, against targets in Formosa to divert Japanese attention away from the landings at Luzon. Thereafter the 58th BW withdrew to its bases in India, and although it was not officially redeployed to the Marianas until February, it did little in its last few weeks of CBI existence. A few minor raids in support of ground forces culminated in an attack against oil storage facilities in Singapore on 29 March and then the campaign ended. In strategic terms it had achieved nothing, for only 49 missions, involving 3058 aircraft sorties, had been flown and only 11,477 tons of bombs had been dropped. As the official USAF historians concluded postwar, the China missions 'did little to hasten the Japanese surrender or to justify the lavish expenditure poured out in their behalf.' Matterhorn had failed, but the experience gained in the process was to be of inestimable value as the B-29s built up their operations from the far more convenient and logical base of the Marianas. The big bombers still had something to prove, but still had to find a role.

Left: Major General Curtis E LeMay.
Below left: B-29s of 468th BG, 58th BW hit the Omura aircraft factory on Kyushu, October 1944.
Below: B-29 of 468th BG over Yawata, July 1944 (note fires in areas of coke ovens, furnaces and shipyards).

EARLY RAIDS FROM M

The Marianas Chain, consisting principally of the islands of Saipan, Tinian and Guam, lies in the central Pacific, occupying a 500-mile arc between latitudes 13 and 21 degrees north. In the context of World War II, it appeared to be an ideal base from which to launch B-29 raids against Japan. The islands were about 1500 miles south-southeast of Tokyo, a range which the B-29s could just about manage. They were relatively invulnerable to enemy counterattack and, most important of all, they could be put on a direct supply route from the United States. In short, they seemed to offer solutions to the majority of B-29 problems experienced in the CBI, except for one crucial factor. When strategic deployment of XX BC was discussed in 1943, the Marianas were firmly under Japanese control.

Suggestions for the seizure of the Marianas were initially put forward by Admiral Ernest King at the Anglo-American Trident Conference in Washington in May 1943, but no action was taken then or two months later at Quebec. With Allied forces locked in a vicious struggle in the Solomons and New Guinea, plans for the occupation of such distant targets must have seemed premature. Instead the AAF planners were obliged to adopt the CBI deployment of the B-29s as put forward by Arnold at Quebec, with all its attendant problems. It was not until September 1943 that the potential of the Marianas as a bomber base was fully realized, and it was this which prompted Arnold to approach the Joint Planning Staff with new ideas. On 4 October he pressed officially for 'the seizure of the Marianas at the earliest possible date, with the establishment of heavy bomber bases as the primary mission.'

This proposal was placed before the Combined Chiefs of Staff at the Cairo Conference in December and after lengthy discussions they decided to incorporate it into an overall offensive Pacific strategy for the coming year. This envisaged two main Allied drives across the ocean toward Japan, one through the center under Nimitz and one from the southwest under MacArthur. Nimitz, whose drive was seen as the more important, was directed to make plans accordingly. He pro-

Below: **Spare R-3350 engines are overhauled in front of a B-29 of 19th BG, 314th BW, Guam, 1945.**

ARIANAS

posed a concentration on nine separate islands – Kavieng, Kwajalein, Manus, Eniwetok, Mortlock, Truk, Saipan, Guam and Tinian – the seizure of which would drive a wedge deep into the enemy defenses and open the way to Japan itself, hopefully by the end of 1944. In the event, Truk was by-passed and left to 'wither on the vine,' enabling the other operations to take place ahead of schedule. As early as March 1944, the JCS was able to set the Marianas invasion for 15 June.

The first of the islands in the chain to be attacked was Saipan. On 11 June a four-day naval and air bombardment began softening up the defenses for an assault landing. On the 15th, the 2nd and 4th Marine Divisions stormed ashore. They were reinforced 24 hours later by the 27th Army Division. After heavy fighting which cost over 3000 American lives (by comparison, the Japanese lost nearly 24,000) the island was effectively cleared by 9 July. This enabled the invasions of Guam and Tinian to go ahead on 20 and 23 July respectively, these islands were declared clear on 9 August. The Americans now had potential bomber bases within range of the entire Japanese mainland.

Before the B-29s could begin operations airfields and support facilities had to be built. Construction work started on Saipan as early as 24 June, while the battle was still raging for possession of the island. Naval Construction Battalions, the celebrated 'Seabees,' concentrated initially upon a former Japanese airstrip called Aslito, soon to be renamed Isley Field after Navy Commander Robert H Isely (unfortunately his name was misspelled at some point and the incorrect version stuck). When the Seabees arrived, Aslito was a short coral strip, just about capable of handling fighter aircraft, and was being used by P-47 Thunderbolts of the 19th Fighter Squadron. They had something like ninety days to transform it into a bomber base for the entire 73rd BW, recently ordered to the Marianas instead of the CBI. As the wing contained the usual four Bombardment Groups (the 497th, 498th, 499th and 500th), each of three squadrons of ten B-29s per squadron, Isley had to be big, with at least two runways, paved to 9000ft and a plethora of support facilities. It was an enormous task and had not been fully completed when the first B-29 touched down on 12 October. Only one runway was capable of taking the bomber – and that was paved to only 6000ft – and there was a total absence of hardstands or buildings. It looked like Chengtu all over again.

Left below: B-29s of 29th BG, 314th BW assume combat formation after taking off from Guam, June 1945.
Below: The bomb-bay doors of this B-29 were hydraulically operated; most crews preferred the more instantaneous electrical system in combat.

The B-29 which arrived on 12 October was piloted by Major General Haywood S Hansell Jr, a man who had been Arnold's chief of staff at 20th AF until August 1944, when he was directed to take command of the newly-activated XX1 Bomber Command, formed specifically for the Marianas operations. His command consisted entirely of the 73rd BW. Another three BWs were still in the process of being formed and the first would not be ready much before the end of the year, and the bombers began to arrive on 18 October. The first was piloted by Brigadier General Emmett (Rosie) O'Donnell, who had replaced Chapman as commander of 73rd BW back in March. By 22 November over 100 aircraft had arrived on Saipan, directly from their training bases.

By that time Hansell had already begun to prepare his forces for their primary mission, that of destroying the Japanese capability to continue the war. Before leaving America he had been told by the JCS that the top priority for the Marianas-based bombers was to destroy the aircraft industry of Japan, and they had supported his preference for high-altitude, daylight precision attacks. However, it was soon apparent that the skill required for such attacks to be successful was not available among the inexperienced crews of 73rd BW. In late October and early November a series of tactical shakedown raids were mounted from Saipan and almost immediately the CBI pattern of problems re-emerged. On 27 October, 18 B-29s were sent against Japanese force targets on Truk; four aborted because of the inevitable engine failures, combat formations were scrappy and the results were officially described as 'poor to fair.' A similar pattern was repeated in two further raids against Truk on 30 October and 2 November. Furthermore, as the Japanese realized what was going on, they added the complication of low-level air raids from Iwo Jima on Isley Field, damaging several B-29s on 2 November. Hansell reacted by ordering retaliatory strikes against Iwo Jima on 5 and 11 November, but again the results were poor. The parallels between these raids and the early ones from Chengtu were obvious to all; the B-29s, beset with problems, were in danger of being dissipated in tactical missions and even then were not enjoying much success.

The outcome was familiar, for Arnold, so acutely aware that the entire autonomous future of the AAF was riding on the Marianas' B-29s now that the Chengtu raids were beginning to fail, pressed Hansell for attacks upon Japan as soon as possible. Hansell, like Wolfe before him in the CBI, was not really ready to oblige. The Saipan base was incomplete (some of the maintenance facilities did not actually arrive until April 1945), the B-29s were experiencing all the usual problems of overheating engines, and the air crews were finding it difficult to settle down to combat conditions. This was due in large measure to Hansell's insistence upon high-altitude, daylight precision attacks, for these presupposed a high level of crew expertise, particularly in formation flying and self-defense. Unfortunately the 73rd BW had done the bulk of its training on radar bombing, with each aircraft having a certain degree of choice about altitude and bombing runs. This had implied that night raids would be flown, so escaping from the danger of enemy interception. When Hansell had announced his choice of tactics the training schedule had been changed, with the result that few crews were really adept at anything. Far from being the surgeon's scalpel which Hansell envisaged and precision bombing required, the 73rd BW was just about capable of becoming a bludgeon, but only if mechanical problems allowed. Arnold seemed incapable of appreciating this.

All this should have been apparent during the shakedown raids against Truk and Iwo Jima and, when this was not the case, it should have become glaringly obvious once the raids against Japan began. The first raid was scheduled for 17 November but the weather, in a preview of problems to come, closed in, grounding the bombers for a week. This breathing space was quite useful from a maintenance point of view – the 73rd BW mechanics used it to fit extemporized cooling baffles to the R-3350s – but it did not prevent the usual run of problems when 111 B-29s finally took off on 24 November. Their target was the Nakajima Aircraft Company's Musashi engine plant, just outside Tokyo, which produced about thirty percent of the engines needed by the Japanese Air Force. It was the first visit to Tokyo by American bombers since Doolittle's raid and was conducted in a glare of publicity.

Above right: Captain R S Steakley in RB-29 *Tokyo Rose* was the first reconnaissance pilot over Tokyo in 1944; hence his DFC.
Above far right: Results of a B-29 fire raid on Hamamatsu, 17 June 1945. Whole blocks of the city have been razed.
Below: B-29s of 497th BG, 73rd BW, prepare for takeoff, late 1944.

1. Kawasaki Ki-45 'Nick' twin-engined fighter dives beneath a B-29 of 497th BG, 73rd BW, over Japan.
2. Sergeant J R Krantz, a waist gunner in 497th BG B-29 *American Maid*, hanging outside the aircraft after a depressurization accident over Japan. He was recovered by his crew colleagues.
3. A typical eleven-man crew pose before an untypical B-29, the nose of which has been severed by a runaway propeller.

The raid began badly as seventeen B-29s aborted due to engine failure and things did not improve as the remainder approached the target at altitudes of 27–32,000ft, for they hit a weather phenomenon at that time unknown – the jet stream. Over Japan, particularly during the winter months, winds of exceptionally high speed roar out of the west at almost exactly the altitudes used by the B-29s. The bombers were therefore bowled along at anything up to 450mph, formations were disrupted and accurate bombing was impossible. To cap it all, the Nakajima plant was covered in patchy cloud and only 24 B-29s dropped their bombs in roughly the right place; the rest merely unloaded over the general urban complex of Tokyo. The target was hardly touched and although the Japanese defenses were poor, one B-29 was deliberately rammed by a fighter aircraft and destroyed. It was not a good start.

Over the next few weeks, Musashi was to be revisited no less than ten times by high-flying B-29s, and their overall lack of success acts as an indication of Hansell's failure. Only ten percent of the damage caused was within the 130 acres of plant area and only two percent of the bomb tonnage dropped actually hit buildings. The Japanese work force suffered only 220 fatalities, a figure which was in fact lower than that suffered by the B-29s, for with forty bombers lost on the eleven raids as a whole, 440 airmen failed to return. The final irony was that in one raid carried out by naval fighters and bombers from Vice-Admiral Marc A Mitscher's Task Force 58 in early February 1945, far more damage was done to Musashi than in all the B-29 strikes put together. A similarly depressing picture emerged from raids against the Mitsubishi engine plant at Nagoya in mid-December. Although the actual damage caused was greater than at Musashi, with some seventeen percent of the complex gutted, B-29 losses to enemy defenses had begun to mount until, by the end of 1944, they were averaging four or five per mission. With eleven men on board each aircraft, few of whom were likely to survive even if they bailed out because the Japanese population felt little sympathy for their plight, the defeat of Japan through aerial bombardment was beginning to seem very expensive indeed. On the precedent of the CBI raids earlier in the year, changes of some description were clearly imminent.

They came in early January 1945 when Arnold, dissatisfied with progress, recalled Hansell and moved LeMay from eastern India to take over XXI BC. Hansell continued to direct operations until LeMay's arrival on 20 January. The results did not improve even when, against his beliefs, he authorized an incendiary raid on Nagoya on 3 January in response to pressure from Arnold, who wanted to see if the Hankow success of 18 December could be repeated elsewhere. High-level, daylight bombing had failed, and Hansell laid the blame on the poor training of the 73rd BW as well as on the problems of mechanical breakdown and Japanese defense.

It is worth noting that in two respects Hansell had laid a firm base upon which LeMay could build. The first concerned the B-29 itself, for many of the persistent engine failures could be attributed to its excessive weight. In mid-January 1945, when the abort rate was running at a staggering 23 percent per mission, a weight reduction program was initiated which, through the removal of one of the bomb bay fuel tanks and a cutback on ammunition carried for the 0.5in machine guns, shaved over 6000lb from each aircraft. Performance instantly improved and when this was coupled with a maintenance centralization reform, whereby Hansell's headquarters controlled the entire maintenance operation instead of it being split between the various Bombardment Groups, B-29 endurance began to lengthen. Thereafter engine life was extended from 200–250 hours to 750 hours and the abort rate

gradually declined. By July 1945 it was down to less than seven percent per operation.

LeMay therefore took over a potentially more effective bomber force in the Marianas than he had done in the CBI, and one which was expanding in size. In January the 313th BW (6th, 9th, 504th and 505th BG), commanded by Brigadier General John H Davies, arrived in the islands. He took over the newly-built North Field on Tinian – the biggest bomber base ever constructed, with four parallel, paved runways, each 8500ft long, and all the attendant base facilities. They were ready to join the campaign by early February, taking part in a high-altitude, daylight attack on Kobe on the 4th. This turned out to be one of the last of such attacks, for although LeMay had not imposed tactical changes on his new command immediately, they were not long delayed. After diverting his B-29s to help in the capture of Iwo Jima LeMay issued his new directive on 19 February. Iwo Jima was an essential island base in the bombing campaign as it could be used to house fighter squadrons capable of escorting the B-29s to Japan as well as act as a useful emergency landing ground midway between the Marianas and the targets. The directive introduced the concept of incendiary raids, placing them above attacks on the aircraft industry in the list of priorities. Mindful of Hansell's failure in producing a precise scalpel, LeMay was accepting the facts of life. Owing to crew inexperience and rushed B-29 development, a bludgeon was all that could be fashioned in the short time available. In crude but simple terms, LeMay was arguing that if the B-29s could not hit the factories exactly, they should be used to burn out the towns which contained and supported them. It was a crucial decision.

These new tactics, still carried out at high altitude and in daylight, were tested in two raids against Tokyo on 25 February and 4 March. The material damage caused was substantial by the record of the recent past – on 25 February alone nearly 28,000 buildings were gutted when 172 B-29s unloaded

Below: 'T - Square - 2': a B-29 of 498th BG, 73rd BW, flies over Tokyo suburbs at low level, May 1945.

Above: The last raid on Kobe, 5th June 1945; after this the target was not deemed worth revisiting.

INTELLIGENCE SUMMARY
FIRST TOKYO BOMBING BY
B-29 A/C of XXI BOM. COM.

DATE of MISSION - 24 Nov. 1944
TARGETS - A/C and Industrial Plants
in Tokyo Area.
TIME OVER TARGET - Aprox. 1230.
ENEMY AIR OPPOSITION - Moderate.
FLAK - Meagre to Moderate.
JAP. A/C DESTROYED IN AIR. - 7
OUR A/C LOST or MISSING - 2
RESULTS - Targets Successfully
Bombed as Planned.

Above: Intelligence summary informs ground crews of the first B-29 raid on Tokyo, 24 November 1944.

450 tons of incendiaries. It was obvious though that far more could be achieved, particularly if concentrated bombing patterns emerged. LeMay analyzed the results carefully and came to three important conclusions, that the effects of the jet stream, cloud cover and high operating altitudes were to blame for the failures. All could be countered, he argued, if high-altitude, daylight attacks were phased out and replaced by low-level, high-intensity incendiary raids, possibly at night. He therefore ordered all the B-29s to be stripped of their General Electric gun systems, leaving only the armament in the tail for defense, loaded up with incendiaries and brought down to an operating altitude of 5–6000ft. This would escape the worst of the jet stream, get the bombers below most of the cloud cover and, as the B-29s would no longer have to struggle up to 30,000ft or above, would save on fuel and engine strain. The air crews were understandably wary because they liked the apparent safety of height and computerized gun systems, but LeMay was of the opinion that the Japanese defenses would be caught unawares, having been organized by now to deal only with high-altitude attacks. Anyway, if the raids could be flown at night, the protection of darkness would undoubtedly reduce casualties. It was a bold approach to the problem, reminiscent of the RAF reaction to daylight losses and lack of results over Germany in 1940–42.

The first raid to use these new techniques was scheduled for the night of 9–10 March against the entire urban complex of Tokyo. As yet another Bombardment Wing had arrived in the Marianas – the 314th (19th, 29th, 39th and 330th BG) under Brigadier General Thomas S Power, stationed at North Field on Guam – LeMay was able to deploy a large number of B-29s. A total of 279 arrived over the target, led by special pathfinder crews who marked a central aiming point, and in a raid which lasted for two hours early on the morning of 10 March the center of Tokyo was devastated. High ground winds gusting up to 28mph fanned the incendiary bursts into a fire-storm of terrifying proportions, sixteen square miles of urban build-

ings were destroyed and nearly 84,000 people died. It was a crippling bludgeon blow to the body, as distinct from the industrial heart of the enemy. Although the loss of fourteen B-29s implied that LeMay's beliefs about ineffective Japanese defenses were wrong, the big bombers had at last begun to make their mark.

Nor was this a purely fortuitous result, for over the next few nights the pattern was successfully repeated, albeit in not quite such a devastating fashion. On 11–12 March 285 B-29s dropped 1700 tons of incendiaries on Nagoya, levelling two square miles of the city for the loss of only one of their number; on 13–14 March eight square miles of Osaka disappeared in a sea of flame; on 16–17 March three square miles of Kobe were gutted; and on 19–20 March, in a return visit to Nagoya, a further three square miles were added to the list of devastation. In all over 120,000 Japanese civilians died in less than two weeks, a relatively small number of B-29s were lost (twenty including those shot down over Tokyo) and the entire strategic bombing project was justified. Arnold was naturally ecstatic and ordered the raids to continue. Unfortunately by 20 March XXI BC had run out of incendiaries (some high-explosive ordnance had been used against both Kobe and Nagoya as stocks ran down) and a pause had to be imposed. Nevertheless the B-29 now had a viable strategic role which could be used to prove the need for future air force autonomy. Up to this time the arguments had been based upon the interwar theories of Mitchell – that the manned bomber could fly with relative impunity over the enemy homeland to destroy precise targets of industrial importance – but the fire raids provided a proven alternative. Using napalm and incendiary clusters, bombers could now impose a high degree of damage on the enemy state. Mitchell had favored the scalpel. The B-29 experience suggested that a bludgeon was all that could be developed under the pressures and problems of war. By 20 March 1945 this had become a highly effective bludgeon, but one which had yet to defeat the enemy single-handed.

THE DESTRUCTION OF

As LeMay awaited the arrival of new incendiary stocks in late March, he was able to devote the B-29s to tactical support missions over the island of Kyushu, designed to prevent Japanese aircraft stationed there from interfering with the imminent invasion of Okinawa. Plans for such support had been finalized on 7 March, before the fire raids began, and it had been decided that the bombers should concentrate upon airfield and support facilities on Kyushu. The first raid took place on 27 March, five days before the Okinawa assault went in, when 151 B-29s hit airstrips at Tachiari and Oita as well as an aircraft plant at Omura. In a series of follow-up strikes all known airfields on Kyushu were destroyed, but the B-29s were ordered to continue their operations throughout April and early May in a desperate attempt to stop kamikaze suicide strikes being launched from Kyushu against American naval forces around Okinawa. In the event, the kamikazes continued to attack, using temporary airstrips in remote locations, and by 11 May Nimitz was forced to admit that the B-29s could not achieve a great deal more. He therefore released them for other operations.

In fact LeMay had never committed his entire force to these strikes – by April 1945 he had over 700 B-29s under his command – and had been able to issue a new fire-raid directive in early April. This gave high priority to the destruction of the aircraft-engine factories at Musashi and Nagoya, but designated selected urban areas for incendiary strikes. These were to be concentrated in the six major cities of Japan – Tokyo, Nagoya, Osaka, Kawasaki, Kobe and Yokohama – with the aim of destroying them and demoralizing their civilian populations.

The raids began on 13 April when 327 B-29s, following the pattern of the earlier incendiary strikes, dropped 2100 tons onto Tokyo's arsenal area and burned out about eleven square miles of the city. Japanese defenses were better organized to deal with night area raids by this time, and seven of the bombers were shot down. Even when these were joined by a further thirteen B-29s, destroyed on 15 April over Tokyo, Kawasaki and Yokohama, the results far outweighed the losses. In addition by mid-April XXI BC had received yet another Bombardment Wing, the 58th, redeployed from the now defunct XX BC in the CBI to West Field on Tinian, and LeMay was able to use 500 bombers in one raid for the first time. He was now of the firm opinion that Japan could be defeated, using air power alone, within six months.

With this aim in mind, he initiated a new series of sustained fire raids in May, beginning on the 14th when 472 B-29s gutted three square miles around and within the Mitsubishi engine factory at Nagoya. Two nights later, a return visit to the city devastated a further four square miles and the first signs of civilian panic began to appear as 170,000 terrified people fled into the surrounding countryside. On 23 and 25 May the B-29s concentrated yet again on Tokyo, and although bomber losses began to rise alarmingly (43 were lost on these two raids alone), the Japanese capital was rapidly becoming a fire-scorched desert. By the end of the month over fifty percent of the city area, some 56 square miles, had been destroyed.

However, the losses were worrying, and in an attempt to confuse the enemy defenses as well as to lure Japanese fighters into an air battle they could not possibly win, a change of tactics was ordered on 29 May. Reverting temporarily to daylight, high-altitude attacks, 454 B-29s appeared over Yokohama escorted by P-51 Mustang fighters from Iwo Jima. The result was a ferocious 'dog-fight' which effectively drew the teeth of the Japanese defending aircraft as 26 were destroyed for the loss of four B-29s and three P-51s. Thereafter, as the Japanese began to hoard what aircraft they had left for a massive, last ditch suicide strike against any Allied invasion force which approached the home islands, air defense of the cities seemed to decline in priority. By June 1945 LeMay was able to report that air interception had lessened considerably and that the B-29s had virtual control of Japanese airspace. This was reflected by the fact that on 5 June the B-29s were able to attack Kobe with such devastating effect that the city was subsequently crossed off the target list as not worth revisiting. Osaka followed suit within ten days. By the end of the month the six major cities in LeMay's April directive had been effectively destroyed, with 105.6 of their combined 257.2 square miles completely devastated. It was an impressive record, particularly when its announcement coincided with the first anniversary of the B-29 strikes upon Japan.

This success, coupled with the ever-growing strength of XXI BC, enabled LeMay to vary his bombing tactics considerably, so increasing Japanese defensive confusion and adding to the general destruction of the enemy. Experiments had in fact begun as early as 7 April, when LeMay had authorized a series of selective high-level precision strikes, using the more experienced crews, and the results were spectacular. The targets were the seemingly indestructible aircraft-engine plants at Musashi and Nagoya. On 7 April 153 B-29s hit the Nagoya complex with about 600 tons of high-explosives, destroying something like ninety percent of the surviving facilities. Five days later 93 B-29s did the same to the Nakajima factory at Musashi. The Japanese aircraft-engine industry had virtually ceased to exist.

APAN

Below left: Incendiary bombs rain down on dockyard facilities at Osaka, 1 June 1945.
Right: The unseen results of the incendiary raids: Japanese school children practice their fire drill.
Below: B-29s of 498th BG, 73rd BW show AN/APQ-13 radomes extended as well as the intermediate tail-fin markings of April 1945.

Such results encouraged LeMay to devote a substantial force of bombers to specific high-priority targets. He chose to concentrate upon Japan's ailing oil-producing and storage facilities and gave the task of their destruction to the newly-arrived 315th BW (16th, 331st, 501st and 502nd BG), commanded by Brigadier General Frank Armstrong and stationed on Northwest Field, Guam. This wing was in fact unique, for it was equipped entirely with the only true variant of the B-29 ever manufactured – the B-29B. Produced at the Bell Aircraft Company's plant at Marietta, Georgia, these aircraft were actually stripped-down versions of the normal B-29, bereft of the General Electric gun system and a variety of other components in order to save weight and increase bomb-carrying capacity. The resultant unladen weight of 69,000lb was a vast improvement, lessening the strain on engines and airframe and enabling the payload to be increased from 12,000 to 18,000lb of ordnance. In addition the B-29Bs were equipped with the new AN/APQ-7 'Eagle' radar sets which gave a much clearer presentation of ground images through a wing-shaped radome slung beneath the fuselage. The crews of the 315th had undergone intensive training for low-altitude, nighttime pathfinder missions, so their navigation and bomb-aiming skills were good. These were proved between 26 June and 10 August when, in a series of strikes against carefully selected targets, they effectively destroyed the oil stocks and production facilities of Japan.

As a final variation of usage LeMay also contributed his B-29s to the extensive mining of Japanese home waters, something which many historians have seen as one of the most decisive campaigns in the Pacific War. Between 27 March and 10 August aircraft, principally of the 313th BW, dropped nearly 13,000 acoustic and magnetic mines in the western approaches to the narrow Shimonoseki strait and the Inland Sea, as well as around the harbors of Hiroshima, Kure, Tokyo, Nagoya, Tokuyama, Aki and Noda. The results were dramatic. All Japanese coastal shipping came to a standstill in April and then, when merchant vessels were ordered to break through the blockade in May, 85 ships totalling 213,000 tons were sunk. After the war was over the United States Strategic Bombing Survey, set up to assess the contribution of aerial bombardment to victory, credited the B-29s with 9.3 percent of the total Japanese shipping loss of 8,900,000 tons.

Below: **A veteran B-29 –** *Look Homeward Angel* **of 6th BG, 313th BW – after a forced landing on Okinawa, August 1945.**

Meanwhile LeMay had not dispensed with incendiary raids, issuing a new directive in mid-June which specified 58 smaller Japanese cities, all with populations of between 100,000 and 200,000, as the targets. On 17 June 450 B-29s flew low-level, night area raids against Kagashima, Omuta, Hamamatsu and Yokkaichi, following them up two nights later with attacks upon Toyohashi, Fukuoka and Shizuoka. The damage was substantial, particularly as by now the bombers were virtually unchallenged in their flights over Japan. Then in late June yet another new technique was introduced. Special leaflets, warning of forthcoming attacks, were dropped over Japanese cities and every third night thereafter the specified urban areas were devastated. The civilian population, faced with this constant proof of American power, began to show signs of panic and the Imperial Cabinet for the first time explored the possibilities of a negotiated end to hostilities. The B-29 had become a highly versatile and awesome weapon of strategic war, and by the beginning of August LeMay was running short of worthwhile targets.

The fact remains, that, despite these continuous and damaging blows to the body of the enemy state, the fire raids, precision strikes and mining operations carried out by the B-29s did not produce the unconditional surrender which the AAF planners had promised. They were certainly contributing enormously to the process of weakening the enemy, but the Allied leaders were still faced with the apparent need to invade the Japanese home islands. It was estimated that this operation would extend the war well into 1946 and probably cost the lives of a million Allied soldiers. It was this above all else that led to the decision in July 1945 to use the new and untested atomic weapons. As the B-29 was the only aircraft capable of acting as a delivery platform, it was about to make its most significant contribution to the history of war.

Experiments in atomic fission had been conducted in a variety of countries before World War II, notably in Germany where the chemist Otto Hahn had described a feasible process of neutron bombardment in 1938, but it was not until the enormous industrial and economic potential of the United States had been mobilized in 1942 that the real work of producing a bomb began. Although this work, carried out under the codename Project Manhattan, did not reach fruition until 1945, it was clear from quite early on that all that

was needed was time, and as early as July 1943 Arnold was requested to provide specially-modified B-29s for flight and bomb-drop tests. Few of the AAF officers involved were told anything beyond the existence of a new weapon. Operating in conditions of enormous secrecy, a team of technical experts was gradually brought together at Wright Field. In December 1943 one of the early production B-29s was withdrawn from the 58th BW and the modification program began.

At first the AAF team could only be provided with very rough dimensions for the new weapon since at this stage even the Manhattan scientists were not sure what it would look like, and attention was concentrated initially upon the bomb bays alone. Aware of the potentially delicate nature of the intended load, the technicians fitted a new H-frame, hoist, carrier assembly and release unit to the B-29. The first drop tests, using dummy bombs of roughly the right dimensions, took place at Muroc, California, on 28 February 1944. These led to the fitting of an entirely new suspension mechanism to

the B-29, while the scientists used the information provided to add several new design features to the projected weapon. Tests resumed in June 1944 and after even more modifications a contract was awarded to a firm in Omaha, Nebraska, to produce a further three of the redesigned B-29s. By this time the scientists were able to provide more accurate dimensions for two types of bomb. One, dependent for its chain reaction upon uranium and nicknamed 'Little Boy,' would be 28in in diameter, 120in long and weigh about 9000lb. The other, using plutonium and called 'Fat Man,' would be 60in in diameter, 128in long and weigh about 10,000lb. Fortunately both these weapons could be lifted and delivered by the modified B-29s; by August the Omaha firm had completed a total of 46 'atomic bombers.'

Meanwhile a special air crew training program had been initiated under the command of Colonel Paul W Tibbetts Jr, a veteran of B-17 operations in Europe and North Africa who was already familiar with the B-29, having been involved in

Above: B-29s of 29th BG, 314th BW on the long haul over the vastness of the Pacific to targets in Japan.
Right: Colonel Paul Tibbetts, commander of 509th CG, poses before *Enola Gay* just prior to takeoff for Hiroshima, 6 August 1945.

Above: **B-29** *Enola Gay* **of 509th CG. Note distinctive tail-fin marking and masked side blister.**

flight testing the machine for over a year. He gathered around him a hand-picked and highly competent staff and in September 1944 took command of the newly-activated 509th Composite Group at a remote air base near Wendover, Utah. The 509th, unique in B-29 history as it contained only one Bombardment Squadron – the 393rd under Major Charles W Sweeney – was a completely self-sufficient unit. It was surrounded in secrecy, with its own engineer, material and troop squadrons as well as a military police contingent. Training began immediately, with test drops of bomb models from high altitude over Inyokern, California, and long overwater navigation flights to Batista Field in Cuba. The 509th was ready for deployment overseas by spring 1945, with the vast majority of its officers and men completely ignorant of its intended role.

Commanders in the Pacific theater were informed of the potential of atomic weapons in February and March 1945, and engineering officers attached to the 509th gained LeMay's full co-operation. Although the unit was to be part of XXI BC in the Marianas its operations were to be strictly controlled from a far higher level of command. Elements of the 509th began to move out from Wendover in early May, and by July the bombers and their support elements were established at North Field, Tinian, the superb, four-runway base only recently completed for the 313th BW. Further bomb-drop tests and long-distance training flights were carried out, causing wry amusement to the battle-hardened veterans of XXI BC, and the modified B-29s were prepared for action. Some were subjected to even more modification when Curtiss electric propellers were fitted. These had reversible pitch to add braking power and sported special blade cuffs which increased airflow, much of which was fed back into the R-3350 engines to aid cooling.

The unit arrived on station only just in time, for early on 16 July the Manhattan scientists test-exploded their first atomic device at Alamogordo in the New Mexico Desert. It was an awe-inspiring success, producing an enormous ball of fire and blast wave which devastated the test site. The news was sent immediately to President Harry S Truman, at that time in Potsdam for the Allied Conference on the future of a now-peaceful Europe. He was fully briefed about potential casual-

ties should Japan be invaded, and had no hesitation in authorizing the use of the new weapons. On 24 July a mission directive was sent to General Carl A Spaatz, commander of the newly-formed US Strategic Air Forces in the Pacific. It ordered the 509th to 'deliver its first special bomb as soon as weather will permit visual bombing after 3 August 1945 on one of the targets: Hiroshima, Kokura, Niigata and Nagasaki.'

Components of 'Little Boy,' the first bomb to be used, had begun to arrive at Tinian on 29 July and by 2 August everything was ready for the attack. That afternoon LeMay's staff made out the necessary field order, specifying Hiroshima as the primary target, with Kokura and Nagasaki as alternatives should bad weather prevent a visual drop. The raid was set to take place on 6 August and Tibbets, who had decided some time before that he would command the attacking B-29, spent the intervening days preparing his crew and aircraft. After the last of their training flights, he directed the unit sign writer to paint his mother's name, *Enola Gay*, beneath the pilot's cabin on the port side of the fuselage.

On 6 August three special reconnaissance F-13As took off from Tinian at 0145 hours to report weather conditions over the primary and secondary targets. Tibbets followed in *Enola Gay* an hour later and during the long outward journey he was cleared for Hiroshima. As Navy weapons expert Captain William Parsons armed the bomb – it had been decided not to do this on the ground at North Field in case of accident – the target was approached and the aiming-point sighted. Once 'Little Boy' had left the bomb bay at 0815, Tibbets pulled the B-29 sharply away in a 155 degree turn to escape the glare and blast he had been warned to expect. His rear-gunner, Technical Sergeant George (Bob) Caron, witnessed the instantaneous death of 78,000 Japanese people, the destruction of some 48,000 buildings and the dawn of a new age.

Despite its devastation the raid did not lead to an immediate Japanese surrender. Poor communications between the remains of Hiroshima and Tokyo, coupled with an understandable lack of comprehension among the Japanese leaders, resulted in a series of cabinet meetings but a lack of consensus about surrender. By 8 August there had still been no official reaction, and the Americans were forced to prepare the plutonium 'Fat Man' – the only remaining atomic device in existence – for a second raid. It was loaded into a B-29 called *Bock's Car*, named after its commander Captain Frederick C

Bock but to be flown on this mission by Major Sweeney. The primary target was specified as Kokura, with Nagasaki as an alternative.

This raid did not run quite as smoothly as the first. As Sweeney approached Kokura early on 9 August, the city was protected by patchy cloud and despite three separate bombing runs the bombardier could not pinpoint the specified aiming feature. Running low on fuel, Sweeney turned for Nagasaki. A few minutes before 1100 hours, the B-29 swung over the new target, also covered with cloud, and released 'Fat Man' on a fleeting sight of the aiming point. A few seconds later Nagasaki disappeared under the now-familiar fire-ball and mushroom cloud. An estimated 35,000 people died.

The Japanese government, rocked by these two demonstrations of American power as well as a Soviet declaration of war on 9 August, realized that the end had come. After consultations with the Emperor, acceptance of Allied terms was wired to the 'Big Three' leaders through Switzerland and Sweden. It took time for the final details to be settled – in fact LeMay's campaign of conventional bombing continued until 14 August, when a record number of 804 B-29s hit targets in Japan – but to all intents and purposes, the war was over. The surrender ceremony took place on 2 September aboard the battleship USS *Missouri* in Tokyo Bay. By that time the bulk of the B-29s had been diverted from errands of death to ones of mercy, dropping food and clothing to the thousands of Allied POWs still in Japanese hands.

Thus, almost exactly three years after its maiden flight, the B-29 had more than justified its costly and difficult development. From the problems of the early months of operations against Japan, the aircraft had rapidly assumed the role of a true strategic bomber, capable of defeating an enemy state virtually on its own. During the Marianas operations, a total of 23,500 individual aircraft sorties had been flown and 170,000 tons of conventional ordnance, as well as two atomic bombs, had been dropped. A total of 371 bombers had been destroyed in the process, but their loss had saved enormous casualties by precluding the need for an invasion of Japan and, as it turned out, had paved the way to USAF autonomy. In 1947 an independent air force was created, based upon the proven ability of atomic-armed bombers to undermine the enemy's capability to wage modern technological war. The B-29s were an integral part of the new Strategic Air Command and although they were quickly superseded by even more powerful aircraft, notably the B-36 and B-50, their war service was far from over. They still had one more campaign to fight.

Left: The awesome mushroom cloud of an atomic explosion; in this case over **Nagasaki, 9 August 1945.**
Below: Japanese Foreign Minister Mamoru Shigemitsu signs the surrender document on board USS *Missouri*, **2 September 1945.**

KOREAN SWANSONG

By 1950 the B-29 was no longer the sophisticated ultra-modern bomber it had seemed eight years earlier. Production had ceased in May 1946, by which time a total of 3960 had been built, and new aircraft, based upon the experiences of World War II and reflecting the new needs of an independent USAF, had begun to appear. Vast numbers of B-29s had been placed in storage. Eighty-eight of these were in fact transferred to the Royal Air Force in 1950, where they became known as 'Washingtons,' and those which remained in USAF Strategic Air Command (SAC) or conventional bombing squadrons rapidly began to look tired and not a little obsolete. Indeed by 1950 they had been redesignated as 'medium' bombers, with their role as the 'very heavy' components of American aerial power being taken over by the B-36 and B-50. Their useful life was clearly nearing its end.

This became irrelevant on 25 June 1950 when North Korean forces, equipped and trained by Communist-Bloc countries, suddenly crossed the 38th parallel into South Korea. A small, bitter war began which was soon to draw in the United States and demand the use of whatever conventional weapons were available. The B-29s of the Far Eastern Air Forces (FEAF), 22 aircraft of the 19th Bomb Group stationed at Anderson Field, Guam, and still a part of 20th Air Force, were the only bombers capable of hitting the Korean peninsula with any effect using conventional ordnance, and their commitment was guaranteed. In the event, they and a number of SAC B-29 Bomb Wings transferred from the United States were to find themselves involved in very little strategic bombing as such, but their contribution over the next three years to the containment of Communist aggression in Korea was to be significant. Despite persistent problems, not only with the aircraft themselves, but also with the roles they were expected to carry out, the B-29s were to prove to be a useful weapon.

They were not committed immediately, however, for American military involvement in Korea was by no means an inevitable result of the North Korean invasion. Korea as a whole had been freed from Japanese occupation in 1945 by Soviet forces from Manchuria in the north and American forces from the Pacific in the south. To prevent unnecessary friction or confrontation the two nascent superpowers had decided, rather arbitrarily, to meet on the 38th parallel. The outcome had been the development of two entirely separate states; the Democratic People's Republic (North Korea) under Premier Kim Il Sung, backed by the Soviets, and the Republic of Korea (South Korea) under Dr Syngman Rhee, ostensibly backed by the United States. The immediate post-war years saw a massive demobilization of American forces and a drift back toward international isolationism. Although the United States was interested in seeing a reunification of Korea through United Nations supervised elections, it was not prepared to insist upon this with force when Kim Il Sung refused to co-operate. The last of the American occupying troops left South Korea in June 1949 and the initial reaction to the North Korean attack a year later was merely to protect US nationals caught in the war zone. It was not until the UN Security Council had voted in favor of supplying aid to the South Koreans on 27 June that General MacArthur, com-

Above: **Bridges over the Han River, destroyed by B-29s in an attempt to stop the North Korean advance, June 1950.**

Above: **A reconnaissance RB-29 of 31st SRS, 1950, at the time of the Korean War.**

manding US forces in Japan, was authorized to commit units to the defense of Syngman Rhee's embattled troops.

At first President Truman restricted US involvement to air elements only, and on 27 June MacArthur ordered General George E Stratemeyer, Commander in Chief of FEAF, to employ his aircraft against any targets of value, particularly troop concentrations and supply dumps, between the front line and the 38th parallel in an attempt to blunt the North Korean advance. When the B-29s flew their first combat mission of this new war, therefore, they were committed to tactical support of the South Korean Army, a role for which they had not been specifically designed. As a result they were thrown into a conflict which was so confused that more formalized and planned bombing policies were impossible to work out. On 28 June four aircraft of the 19th BG flew over Korea, searching for and destroying targets of opportunity on rail routes to the north of Seoul, the already-fallen South Korean capital. A more definite policy seemed to be emerging

the next day, when, on direct orders from MacArthur, a further nine B-29s began to hit North Korean airfields, but the pressures of a fast-moving war doomed this campaign to an early grave. As North Korean forces concentrated on the Han River in preparation for a major push southward, the bombers were diverted to attacking them, with predictably poor results. This was to be a constantly recurring pattern over the next three years, as the USAF planners on the one hand searched for a role which the B-29s could carry out consistently, while the land commanders on the other insisted upon tactical close support whenever the situation demanded. It was to result in a basic misuse of the strategic bomber and an inconclusive end to the B-29s combat career.

At least the USAF could attempt an independent line, and one of the first steps in this direction was the setting up of a command structure to control B-29 operations. This took place on 8 July when a special FEAF Bomber Command was authorized under Major General Emmett O'Donnell, the

Below: **B-29s of SAC 22nd BW fly toward their targets in Korea, September 1950.**

Above: **B-29s of SAC 22nd BW release 500lb bombs over Korean targets, September 1950.**

erstwhile leader of the 73rd BW in the Marianas. He established his headquarters at Yokata, Japan, and in addition to the 19th BG, was given two Bomb Wings – the 22nd and 92nd – transferred temporarily from SAC on 3 July by USAF Chief of Staff General Hoyt S Vandenberg. Together with six RB-29 long-range reconnaissance aircraft belonging to SAC's 31st Strategic Reconnaissance Squadron on Okinawa, 24 weather-reconnaissance WB-29s and four SB-29 'Superdumbo' rescue machines, this gave O'Donnell a theoretical strength of approximately 100 aircraft. Unfortunately his first brief came from MacArthur who directed him to use them north of the Han River, principally against targets of opportunity on the battlefield. This role should have been carried out by fighter bombers.

Understandably the results were disappointing and by 18 July Vandenberg was complaining to MacArthur that this was no way to treat the B-29s. MacArthur agreed and diverted the bombers to interdiction raids nearer the 38th parallel, designed to cut off the North Koreans in the south from their sources of supply. This was still not a worthy role for the strategic bombers, but at least it was a more formalized approach to their use. Interdiction Campaign No 1 was duly initiated on 4 August and O'Donnell was for the first time given definite target priorities. Between 4 and 10 August the B-29s hit a variety of marshalling yards and rail complexes in North Korea in an attempt to disrupt supplies, but once again the results were poor, chiefly because of a lack of prestrike intelligence information. As a result between 12 and 20 August the emphasis was shifted to a number of strategic road and rail bridges north of the 37th parallel. The majority of these were destroyed, even though they were of extremely strong construction, and the B-29s had to evolve entirely new combat techniques using unsatisfactory weapons. Both the 22nd and 92nd BWs, used to training for atomic strikes at very high altitude and equipped with B-29s which were only capable of delivering 500lb bombs, were not really suited to the

task at all, while the 19th BG, although capable of using 1000 and 2000lb weapons, experienced tremendous problems. One particular railroad bridge at Seoul, assigned to the 19th, in fact took three weeks to knock down, with strikes organized on every single day. Nevertheless by the end of August, O'Donnell could report the complete destruction of 37 of the 44 bridges involved in the campaign, with the remaining seven unusable.

USAF planners have never been entirely satisfied with this emphasis upon tactical strikes, however, preferring a proper strategic bombing campaign against North Korean industry, something which was initially pressed for in early July. Vandenberg offered to send two more SAC Bomb Wings to Japan, the 98th and 307th, and this was probably the deciding factor; in late July he was authorized to begin the necessary planning. SAC Intelligence, using RB-29s of the 31st SRS, quickly earmarked five major industrial centers for attack: the North Korean capital of Pyongyang (a source of armaments and aircraft as well as an important rail center), Wonsan (oil refineries around a major sea port), Hungnam (chemical and metallurgical industries), Chongjin (iron foundries and rail yards) and Rashin (a naval base with oil storage facilities). Other targets of secondary importance were also listed, including five east-coast hydroelectric power complexes. It was obvious that enough targets existed to justify a strategic campaign, particularly as the majority were conveniently concentrated in the northeast. It looked as if the B-29s could be used in their proper role.

The raids began on 30 July when, in three separate but co-ordinated precision, daylight attacks the Hungnam industrial complex was flattened, and this success was maintained against the other primary targets as enthusiasm for the venture grew in Washington and Tokyo. Indeed by early September O'Donnell was able to report the destruction of all known industrial facilities in the North with the exception of those at Rashin which, after one B-29 raid, had been deleted from the target list by the President himself. As Rashin was only seventeen miles from the Soviet border it was felt that a slight bombing error might escalate the conflict unnecessarily. It was a remarkable achievement nonetheless, justifying the USAF insistence and proving the continued power of the B-29 when assigned the relevant tasks. O'Donnell was already moving on to his secondary targets – the first raid in fact took place on 26 September against the Fusen hydroelectricity plant – when the entire course of the war was dramatically altered. For a variety of reasons the B-29s were never again to hit strategic targets.

The initial cancellation of the strategic campaign came about because most of the targets in North Korea were actually captured by UN forces in October 1950. A bold amphibious landing at Inchon and an advance eastward to Seoul in late September threatened to cut the North Koreans off from their homeland. An Allied offensive from Pusan added to the pressure and the North Koreans began a retreat which, harried by constant air strikes, soon degenerated into a rout. South Korean forces crossed the 38th parallel on 1 October, Pyongyang fell eighteen days later and a general United Nations advance toward the Chinese border on the Yalu River met little opposition. Stratemeyer diverted many of the B-29s to tactical strikes in what appeared to be the dying moments of a successful land campaign; strategic bombing became unnecessary and FEAF Bomber Command was disbanded on 27 October, with the 22nd and 92nd BWs returning to SAC duties in the United States. Victory seemed assured.

However, the war was far from over, for as the UN forces approached the Yalu, Chinese units could be seen massing to

Above: **B-29s, possibly of SAC 307th BW, attack a chemical plant at Hungnam during the strategic raids of late July 1950.**

Above: **B-29 of SAC 98th BW salvoes both bomb bays simultaneously over a North Korean target, 13 July 1951.**

the north and war supplies began to pour over the river to sustain the North Koreans. On 1 November Chinese MiG-15 jet fighters appeared for the first time in direct opposition to the USAF, and FEAF Bomber Command was hastily reformed to face the new threat. By now the politicians had begun to realize the likely consequences of escalation, not only with China but also with the Soviet Union, and a conscious restraint in the use of military force – to be called limited war when viewed in retrospect in the late 1950s – seemed advisable. One of the most important aspects of this restraint directly affected the B-29s, for at no time after November 1950 was their use in a strategic role against the Chinese homeland so much as contemplated. The USAF planners were restricted in their operations to the Korean peninsula alone. Although certain industrial targets could be found later in the war, after the Chinese onslaught had pushed the UN forces back below the 38th parallel, their destruction could never affect the true sources of enemy war supplies, safe in the restricted areas of China. The B-29s were forced by political and military necessity to become tactical aircraft.

This was made obvious as early as November 1950 when O'Donnell was ordered to concentrate his forces against the Yalu bridges which were being used to carry supplies from China into North Korea. Between 8 and 25 November the B-29s hit the southern approaches to these targets (to drop bombs on the northern spans would have been an attack upon Chinese territory) at Sinuiju, Hyesanjin, Uiju, Manpojin and Chongsonjin. Some success was achieved – O'Donnell reported a 65 percent destruction rate – but this was illusory. Many of the broken spans were replaced by pontoons which were only used at night. The small-yield bombs tended not to do the damage which was necessary and the Chinese build up of supplies and troops in the North continued virtually unchecked. In addition the B-29s had begun to suffer casualties; one bomber was shot down and ten others badly damaged during these attacks.

The general lack of effect was felt on 25 November when hordes of Chinese troops fell upon the advancing UN forces and, in a series of extremely costly battles, pushed them back to the 38th parallel. The B-29s, like every other available aircraft, flew close support missions in a desperate attempt to stop the flood, but it was not until the end of December that the line began to stabilize. The situation was now much as it had been before Inchon, with the exception that a strategic bombing campaign was impossible, and the B-29s were soon reverting to the previous emphasis upon interdiction. A sporadic campaign took place against rail targets in the North in late December and early January, but a Communist New Year Offensive, which pushed the Allies even further southward, soon necessitated a return to close support.

As this storm was weathered, again at high cost to the land forces, so the planners began to search for a definite B-29 targeting policy, if only to ensure that the tremendous strike potential of the bombers could be concentrated against worthwhile enemy targets. From the map it was obvious that the key area of Chinese supply build up was in the northwest of Korea, but this was also the area containing MiG bases and anti-aircraft defenses. If the B-29s were to be used, they could not go alone, so in what became known as Interdiction Campaign No 4, instigated in February 1951, they were provided with fighter escorts. The early raids were disastrous. The F-86 Sabre jet fighters, the only aircraft capable of taking on the MiG-15s in a sustained campaign, were not yet fully operational in Korea. The early strikes were escorted by F-80C Shooting Stars and F-84E Thunderjets, neither of which were effective. In addition co-ordination between the bomber and fighter commanders was poor, and it was not unknown for the B-29s to go in alone, with predictable results. By 12 April, with three B-29s shot down and ten badly damaged, Stratemeyer called off the raids and diverted the bombers once again to close support, this time against Communist air bases around the 38th parallel.

Concern over the lack of results in this phase of operations was not alleviated by the fact that new bombing techniques and weapons, designed to solve some of the problems already experienced in interdiction strikes, had been used. Up to early 1951, in the absence of organized enemy defenses, the B-29s had been able to make numerous, unhurried bombing runs against a specific target at altitudes as low as 10,000ft. Once the Chinese became involved and both fighters and anti-aircraft guns appeared, this had become virtually suicidal. The raids on northwest Korea had therefore been put in at 20,000ft with the bombers flying in defensive formations ostensibly escorted by fighters. It was worrying that, even then, they had been a poor match for the enemy defenses.

Similarly, a range of new weapons, designed to improve both hitting power and accuracy, had been seen to fail. These were radio-controlled bombs, dropped from an ordinary B-29 and then guided onto the target by the bombardier. The earlier versions, known as 'Razons' because their controller could alter **R**ange and **AZ**imuth **ON**ly once they left the aircraft, proved to be moderately successful (the 19th BG destroyed fifteen bridges with them in late 1950 and early 1951), but had the disadvantage of being a mere 1000lb each. Given this, the next generation, known as 'Tarzons' and weighing 2000lb each, promised to be an effective addition to the United States' arsenal. Unfortunately they were not. When carried by a B-29 nearly two-thirds of the Tarzon protruded outside the bomb bay and they proved to be unwieldy. In the end they were infinitely more dangerous to the bomber crew than the enemy. They were withdrawn from service in late April 1951 after at least two B-29s had been destroyed trying to ditch their bombs in the sea. The Tarzons, full of unstable RDX explosive from the end of World War II, exploded as soon as they hit the water. All told, thirty of these weapons were dropped over Korea, but as only six bridges were destroyed in the process, they represented yet another dead end in the seemingly endless search for a viable B-29 role.

The important area of northwest Korea was not revisited by the B-29s until the end of December 1951, for, in a decision reminiscent of that made by the 8th AAF in Europe in 1943, USAF planners decided to concentrate upon the destruction of Communist air power before moving on to a more vigorous bombing policy. The B-29s had an important part to play in this new move, for they were to act as bait, attacking Communist air bases throughout the North and forcing the MiGs to enter battle with escorting fighters. Between 13 and 27 October the raids went in, but the results were poor. The Communists took to dispersing their MiG squadrons far and wide, even using temporary grass strips on occasion, so that USAF Intelligence could not keep track of their movements and B-29 losses were heavy. By 27 October five of the bombers had been destroyed and a further twenty badly damaged. The raids were quickly suspended and replaced by nighttime attacks using small numbers of B-29s equipped with Shoran (**SHO**rt **RAN**ge) navigation radar which was used to pinpoint small targets with remarkable accuracy. Some success was achieved and these raids continued for the remainder of the war, although as night fighters and radar-controlled defenses began to be experienced, losses did mount alarmingly. On 10 June 1952, for example, four Shoran B-29s suddenly found themselves being tracked by radar-controlled searchlights over Sinuiju. Night fighters homed in and two of the bombers went down in flames, with a third so badly damaged that it barely reached the UN lines before crash landing. The use of B-29s as night intruder bombers was clearly not the answer.

Meanwhile more concentrated attempts at interdiction had

Above: **Aftermath of a B-29 raid on the Chosan nitrogen fertilizer factory, November 1950.**
Top: **Results of a raid on the Chongjin iron foundries, August 1950.**

begun to achieve a small measure of success. On 25 August 1951 35 B-29s of the 19th BG and 98th and 307th BWs had hit the marshalling yards at Rashin (reassigned by Truman to the bombers in light of their importance) in the first of a series of sustained attacks against rail centers. In August and September they concentrated on the north-south rail lines of North Korea with B-29s hitting bridges at Pyongyang, Sonchon, Sunchon, Sinanju and Huichon, but this was soon seen to be indecisive as the Communists quickly repaired or by-passed the break in their supply chain. It was not until more concentrated attacks on specific choke points had been initiated that there was any hope of success. For 44 days, beginning on 26 January 1952, B-29s in close co-operation with other US aircraft dropped nearly 4000 500lb bombs on the one unfortunate village of Wadong where the lateral rail route of North Korea entered a potentially vulnerable defile. Enough damage was inflicted for this new bombing policy to be formalized in early March under the codename Operation Saturate but, again, heavy losses coupled with Communist ingenuity and a lack of suitable targets tended to undermine the effects. The B-29 role had not been found after nearly two years of war.

FEAF planners were well aware of this, and in spring 1952 they proposed the nearest thing they could find to a strategic campaign in a desperate attempt to justify the mounting cost of bomber operations – sustained attacks upon North Korean hydroelectricity facilities. By 28 April the necessary authorization had been gained and four complexes were earmarked for destruction, at Sui-Ho, Fusen, Choshin and Kyosen. The campaign was to be a co-ordinated USAF effort, with the B-29s

Above: **Symbol of air power: a FEAF B-29 flies over an Allied anti-aircraft position, Korea 1952.**

committed to nighttime, Shoran-guided strikes after fighter bombers had gone in during the day. In the event, even the United States Navy contributed with carrier-borne aircraft from Task Force 77 off the coast of Korea. The raids began on 24 June, with the B-29s going in for the first time that night against Choshin. By the 27th it was estimated that nine-tenths of North Korean power supplies had been destroyed.

This success swiftly led to the adoption of a more general bombing policy, based upon the twin characteristics of concentration and co-ordination. The idea was that if selected targets of military importance could be located and then destroyed in a storm of aerial assault, the Communists might be persuaded to agree to an armistice, the negotiations for which had been going on for nearly eighteen months. The first and, as it turned out, the biggest of these raids took place on 11 July against thirty different targets in Pyongyang and the campaign continued over the next few weeks with similar intensive strikes against Sungho-Ri, Choshin, Sindok and Sinuiju. The B-29s contributed to most of these and their gradually-improving nighttime techniques were shown to good effect on 30 September when 45 of them wiped out the Namsan-Ri chemical plant, but enemy defenses were still taking a significant toll. As the raids continued, between November 1952 and January 1953 five B-29s fell victim to night fighters and three more were severely damaged. Only after the deployment of USAF night fighters, especially the F3D-2 Skynight, did losses decrease. Even then it was apparent that the B-29 could never be expected to mount a campaign against North Korea on its own. Only within the protective body of the USAF as a whole could the bomber hope to survive. This fact was reinforced in May 1953, two months before an armistice was eventually signed, when the B-29s could do nothing more than contribute to the successful destruction of North Korean irrigation dams. The targets were virtually strategic, but the bombers could never have hit them alone.

Thus when the Korean War ended on 27 July 1953, the B-29 was quite obviously an obsolete weapon. Its contribution to the United Nations' cause was undoubtedly significant; in 37 months of conflict over 21,000 aircraft sorties had been flown by the B-29 crews, nearly 167,000 tons of bombs had been dropped and 34 of the bombers had been lost (sixteen to enemy fighters, four to flak and fourteen to other causes). However, the original *raison d'être* of the machine had not been satisfied. This was partly due to a lack of strategic targets caused by the restraints of limited war, but it was also a result of tremendous advances in aerial technology which left the B-29 behind. The aircraft belonged to the 1940s, to an age before the jet fighter, radar-controlled defenses and superpower confrontation. It had more than justified its development in 1945 over the skies of Japan, but by 1950 it was almost an anachronism, awaiting retirement and totally unsuited to the rigors of another war. It is certainly no coincidence that as soon as the Korean War ended the USAF accelerated its program of bomber re-equipment, culminating in the delivery of the first jet-engined B-52s in June 1955. The Superfortress gave way to the Stratofortress and their very names indicate the rapid and far-reaching technological strides which had taken place. The B-29 contributed to containment in Korea, but this was not a fitting end to the aircraft's career. Its true worth lay in 1945, not in 1950. It belonged to the total war conditions of the conflict with Japan, not to the infinitely more subtle and potentially dangerous climate of a Cold War.

APPENDICES

1. B-29 Specifications

A. Normal B-29

Applicable to all 1620 B-29s built by the Boeing Aircraft Company at their Wichita, Kansas, plant between September 1943 and October 1945; to 357 B-29s built by the Bell Aircraft Corporation at Atlanta (Marietta), Georgia, between February 1944 and January 1945; and to 536 B-29s assembled by the Glenn L Martin Company at Omaha, Nebraska, between January 1944 and September 1945.

Span	141ft 2in
Length	99ft
Height	27ft 9in (tail fin)
Wing area	1736 sq ft
Weights	Empty: 70,140lb
	Loaded: 135,000lb with 12,000lb bomb load
Powerpack	Four Wright R-3350-23 Cyclone 18-cylinder radials, each with a pair of General Electric B-11 superchargers to give 2200 brake horsepower at takeoff
Propellers	Four-blade Hamilton Standard Hydromatics (16ft 7in diameter) with constant-speed governors and hydraulic operation for pitch change and feathering. Engine gear ratio was 0.35 (that is, the propeller turned at just over one-third of the engine revolutions, so at 2800 engine rpm the propeller was turning at 980rpm)

(Boeing introduced a new R-3350-41, with baffles and oil crossover pipes for improved cooling, on production block 50; both Martin and Bell followed suit on block 20. All three companies had begun to use R-3350-57 engines by the end of the production run. Both new types of engine continued to use the Hamilton propellers but some B-29s were fitted with Curtiss electric propellers, which enjoyed reversible pitch and blade cooling cuffs, toward the end of World War II)

Maximum range	3250 miles at 25,000ft with full fuel and 5000lb bomb load

(This was raised to 4100 miles under the same load conditions by the addition of auxiliary fuel tanks in the bomb bays of later models)

Practical operational radius	1600 miles, rising to 1800 miles after engine and fuel improvements
Maximum ferry range	5600 miles, rising to 6000 miles after improvements
Maximum speed	375mph at 25,000ft (although speeds in excess of 450mph were recorded in the jet stream over Japan in 1944–45)
Normal cruising speed	200–250mph
Fuel-load capacity	8198 US gallons on early models, carried in four wing-tanks. Increased to 9548 US gallons after the installation of extra tanks in the wing center section on Boeing production block 25. Bell incorporated the same on block 5; all Martin B-29s had them as standard fit. Under operational conditions a B-29 would carry 6988 US gallons only if the semipermanent fuel tanks in one of the two bomb bays were taken out
Rate of climb	38 minutes to 25,000ft at 110,000lb gross weight
Service ceiling	31,850ft

Bomb-load capacity	5000lb over 1600 mile radius at high altitude; 12,000lb over 1600-mile radius at medium altitude; 20,000lb maximum over short distances at low altitude. High explosive and incendiary bombs carried, either exclusively or mixed, depending on type of raid
Armament	Ten 0.5in machine guns and one 20mm cannon. Cannon and two 0.5in in the tail, two 0.5in in each of the four remotely-controlled power turrets (forward and aft dorsal, forward and aft ventral) which made up the General Electric computerized gun system

(The forward dorsal turret was increased to four 0.5in machine guns on Boeing production block 40 to increase forward protection. Bell followed suit on block 10, all Martin B-29s had this as standard fit. Similarly, the 20mm cannon was deleted on Boeing production block 55, Bell block 25 and Martin block 25. Its trajectory, totally different from that of the machine guns, had made aiming difficult in combat conditions)

Crew	Eleven men comprising:
	Aircraft Commander (sometimes termed the Command Pilot)
	Pilot (sometimes termed the Co-Pilot)
	Bombardier
	Navigator
	Flight Engineer
	Radio Operator
	Radar Operator
	Central Fire Control Gunner
	Left Side Gunner
	Right Side Gunner
	Tail Gunner

The first six were housed in the forward pressurized cabin, connected by a 34in diameter tube to the next four in the mid-fuselage pressurized area. The tail gunner, in his own completely separate pressurized turret, was in the rear. The Aircraft Commander, Pilot, Bombardier, Navigator and Flight Engineer were all officers, the remainder enlisted men, although the post of Flight Engineer was gradually opened to suitably qualified enlisted men as World War II progressed

Crew size was occasionally increased to thirteen under World War II operational conditions, with the addition of two radar/radio experts (known as 'Ravens') to man the increasingly sophisticated radar and ECM (electronic countermeasures) equipment

Radar equipment	AN/APN-4 Loran (**LO**ng **RAN**ge) constant-beam navigation aid was fitted on early models, being replaced by a more sophisticated AN/APN-9 system during World War II
	AN/APQ-13 radar bombing-navigational aid in retractable radome located between the two bomb bays. Designed to give a radar image of the ground

(Most operational B-29s carried and distributed 'Chaff,' sometimes called 'Window' — metallic foil strips, cut to the exact wavelength of enemy radar, which would saturate and blurr their screens during target approach)

Above right: **Standard B-29 in flight.**
Right: **A B-29 is towed to dispersal.**

B. B-29A

Outwardly there was little noticeable difference between the normal B-29 and the B-29A, the main changes being concentrated in the area of wing construction. Specifications for the B-29A were limited to the 1119 aircraft built at the Boeing plant at Renton, Washington, between January 1944 and May 1946. In the normal B-29 the wing was manufactured as an integral part of the fuselage; in the B-29A a stub center-section was built and then the wing was constructed in seven sections around it. This left room for three wing fuel tanks instead of the normal four, so fuel-load capacity was reduced.

Span	142ft 3in
Length	as normal B-29
Height	as normal B-29
Wing area	1738 sq ft
Weights	Empty: 71,360lb
	Loaded: 135,000lb with 12,000lb bomb load
Engines	as normal B-29, with new R-3350 designs added at much the same time
Propellers	as normal B-29
Maximum range	4000 miles at 25,000ft with full fuel and 5000lb bomb load
Practical operational radius	1800 miles
Maximum ferry range	6000 miles
Maximum speed	as normal B-29
Normal cruising speed	as normal B-29
Fuel-load capacity	9288 US gallons after installation of semipermanent bomb-bay tanks
Rate of climb	as normal B-29
Service ceiling	about 33,000ft
Bomb-load capacity	as normal B-29
Armament	as normal B-29. Four-gun forward dorsal turret installed and 20mm tail cannon deleted on production block 20
Crew	as normal B-29
Radar equipment	as normal B-29

(Some early B-29As were also characterized by the installation of pneumatically operated bomb-bay doors which could be snapped shut in less than a second. Before this the doors had been hydraulically operated, with normal closing speed of seven seconds. By early 1945 all B-29s, normal as well as A and B variants, had pneumatic doors as standard fit)

C. B-29B

Applicable to 311 B-29s built by the Bell Aircraft Corporation at their Marietta plant between January and September 1945. The B-29Bs were basically stripped down versions of the normal B-29, with the General Electric computerized gun system deleted and new radar aids added. Most were issued to the 315th BW in the Marianas in 1945

Span	as normal B-29
Length	as normal B-29
Height	as normal B-29
Wing area	as normal B-29
Weights	Empty: 69,000lb
	Loaded: 137,000lb with 18,000lb bomb load
Powerpack	as normal B-29, although the majority had the R-3350-41 as standard fit
Propellers	as normal B-29
Maximum range	4200 miles at 10,000ft with full fuel and 18,000lb bomb load
Practical operational radius	1800 miles

Maximum ferry range	4000 miles
Maximum speed	364mph at 25,000ft
Normal cruising speed	210–225mph
Fuel-load capacity	6988 US gallons, the bomb-bay tanks not being standard fit
Rate of climb	33 minutes to 20,000ft at 110,000lb gross weight
Service ceiling	32,000ft
Bomb-load capacity	20,000lb (although with a mix of HE and incendiaries, this could be increased to 22,800lb)
Armaments	Two or three 0.5in machine guns in the tail, with provision for two 0.5in in the mid-fuselage pressurized area
Crew	Seven or eight men (the Right and Left Side Gunners were not carried, the Central Fire Control Gunner occasionally acted as an observer and the Bombardier's duties could be taken over by the Radar Operator)
Radar equipment	AN/APQ-7 'Eagle' bombing-navigational aid, housed in retractable radome between the bomb bays and designed to give improved presentation of ground images

D. Boeing 'Washington'

Name applicable to 88 B-29s and B-29As taken out of USAF storage in 1950 and issued to Royal Air Force bombing squadrons under the American military aid to Europe program at the beginning of the Cold War period. Designed to fill the RAF heavy bomber gap between the rapidly aging Avro Lincolns and the still-to-be-developed 'V' bomber jet series. In use between 1950 and early 1958 with Nos 15, 35, 44, 57, 90, 115, 149 and 207 Squadrons, Bomber Command. Specifications as for B-29 and B-29A, except that the RAF usually operated a crew of ten men only, deleting the role of Aircraft Commander, absorbing his duties into those of the Pilot

E. USAAF and USAF operational variants

(a) The atomic B-29s
Specifications as for normal B-29, but incorporating strengthened bomb bays and suspension systems. Ventral area painted white to minimize glare damage. B-29s of USAF Strategic Air Command all of this type post-1947

(b) F-13A and RB-29 reconnaissance aircraft
World War II and USAF versions respectively – these were stripped down B-29s with a service ceiling in excess of 35,000ft. Equipped with a plethora of cameras, especially in bomb-bay areas, they were used for pre- and post-operation reconnaissance over both Japan and Korea. Weather reconnaissance versions, used in the Korean War, were designated WB-29s

(c) SB-29A 'Superdumbo'
Rescue aircraft developed to aid ditched B-29s on the long overwater flights between the Marianas and Japan, 1945. Basic B-29, but with extra crewmen as observers, emergency gear and, most noticeably, a lifeboat slung under the forward fuselage. No armament carried. Continued in use post-World War II

2. Order of Battle, 20th Air Force, 1944–45

Bombard-ment Wing	Bombard-ment Groups	Bombardment Squadrons	Date when became operational
58	40	25, 44, 45 (395)	5 June 1944
	444	676, 677, 678 (679)	
	462	768, 769, 770 (771)	
	468	792, 793, 794 (795)	
73	497	869, 870, 871	28 October 1944
	498	873, 874, 875	
	499	877, 878, 879	24 November 1944
	500	881, 882, 883	11 November 1944
313	6	24, 39, 40	27 January 1945
	9	1, 5, 99	25 January 1945
	504	398, 421, 680*	16 January 1945
	505	482, 483, 484	30 December 1944
314	19	28, 30, 93	12 February 1945
	29	6, 43, 52	15 February 1945
	39	60, 61, 62	6 April 1945
	330	457, 458, 459	12 April 1945
315	16	15, 16, 17	16 June 1945
	331	355, 356, 357	1 July 1945
	501	21, 41, 485	16 June 1945
	502	402, 411, 430	30 June 1945
	509 CG	393	1 July 1945

The Bombardment Squadrons of 58th BW in brackets were all disbanded in September–October 1944.

*680 BS did not join 504th BG until June 1945.

A note on aircraft markings

In common with most aircraft types, B-29s were relatively devoid of markings when first issued to individual squadrons. The US national markings, the 'star and bar,' appeared on the top of the port mainplane and beneath the starboard, as well as on both sides of the mid-fuselage section, aft of the gunners' blisters. The manufacturer's hull serial number was painted on both sides of the tail fin. It was not until the aircraft was allocated to its squadron that more distinctive markings, designed to show at a glance what squadron, group and wing it belonged to, began to be applied. The form of these markings appears to have differed in the CBI and Pacific theaters and to have been changed in the latter in early 1945.

The CBI markings

The four Bombardment Groups of 58th BW appear to have used colors and designs to distinguish themselves, and although it is sometimes difficult to be precise, the following list can be compiled from photographic evidence:

Group	Tail marking
40th	Four horizontal tail stripes and tip
444th	Three vertical rudder stripes
462nd	Bellyband, aft of national marking on fuselage
468th	Two diagonal stripes on the rudder

Within each BG, the individual Bombardment Squadrons were distinguished by the color of their group marking – red, green, yellow and blue being the usual ones – perhaps in order of seniority within the group. Thus the 45th BS of 40th BG would have four yellow horizontal stripes and tip to the rudder; the 794th BS of 468th BG, two yellow diagonal rudder stripes. This squadron color was usually repeated on the engine cowls, propeller bosses and blade tips and even, occasionally, the wheel hubs. The aircraft number within the squadron appeared either on the tail or forward fuselage, and it was not unknown for an individual aircraft letter also to be painted on the fin. The 444th BG adopted a diamond tail marking in late 1944 in addition to the rudder stripes, within which the aircraft number appeared.

The Pacific markings

When B-29s arrived in the Marianas a new system of marking appeared, based upon geometric shapes and letters. Throughout the campaign, the Bombardment Wings were distinguished by the following designs:

58th	A triangle
73rd	An uncolored square
313th	A circle
314th	A dark colored square
315th	A diamond
509th	An arrow, pointing forward, within a circle

In addition, each Bombardment Group had its own letter, and although again it is difficult to be precise, the list of these would seem to be:

Bombardment Group	Letter
40th	(C?)
444th	N
462nd	U
468th	S
497th	A
498th	T
499th	V
500th	Z
6th	R
9th	X
504th	E
505th	W
19th	M
29th	O
39th	P
330th	K
16th	B
331st	(H?)
501st	Y
502nd	(J?)

Before about mid-April 1945 a typical fin marking would consist of three separate items, with the BG letter at the top, the BW geometric shape in the center and the individual aircraft number at the bottom. Because of this, many B-29 crews referred to their aircraft by this code. Thus 'Z – square – 50' would denote the B-29 with the squadron number 50, belonging to the 500th BG of 73rd BW

As more aircraft arrived in the Marianas, however, it did become confusing to use such an elaborate code, and in April 1945 the tail markings were ordered to consist just of the BG letter, painted as large as the fin would allow. This gave no indication of BW, so within a few weeks this was altered again to the BG letter within the BW geometric shape, also as large as possible on the tail fin. Thus the letter R within a circle denoted an aircraft of 6th BG of 313th BW; an uncolored M within a dark square one of the 19th BG of 314th BW. Aircraft numbers now appeared on the aircraft nose and engine cowls.

Throughout these changes squadrons appear to have been distinguished by color – red, green and yellow, perhaps in order of seniority – usually on engine cowls, propeller bosses and blade tips.

3. Chain of Command, B-29 Operations, 1944–45

Joint Chiefs of Staff

20th Air Force
(General Henry H Arnold)

US Strategic Air Forces, Pacific (from June 1945)
(General Carl A Spaatz)

XX BC
Lt Gen Kenneth B Wolfe, Nov 1943–July 1944
Maj Gen Curtis E LeMay, Aug 1944–Jan 1945

XXI BC
Maj Gen Haywood S Hansell, Jr
Aug 1944–Jan 1945
Maj Gen Curtis E LeMay,
Jan–Aug 1945

58TH BW
May 1944–April 1945
Brig Gen La Verne G Saunders

58th BW	**73rd BW**	**313th BW**	**314th BW**	**315th BW**	**509th CG**
from April 1945	Oct 1944	Jan 1945	Apr 1945	June 1945	July 1945
Brig Gen La Verne	Brig Gen Emmett	Brig Gen John	Brig Gen	Brig Gen Frank	Col Paul W
G Saunders	O'Donnell	H Davies	Thomas S Power	Armstrong	Tibbetts, Jr

4. B-29 Losses, April 1944–August 1945

A. XX Bomber Command

Year and Month	Combat Losses	Non-combat Losses	Total
April 1944	—	7	7
May	—	5	5
June	10	8	18
July	3	5	8
August	14	5	19
September	3	7	10
October	5	16	21
November	19	2	21
December	16	6	22
January 1945	4	3	7
February	4	2	6
March	2	1	3
	80	67	147

B. XXI Bomber Command

Year and Month	Combat Losses	Non-combat Losses	Total
November 1944	4	5	9
December	21	6	27
January 1945	27	—	27
February	26	3	29
March	34	—	34
April	57	1	58
May	88	3	91
June	44	7	51
July	22	5	27
August	11	7	18
	334	37	371

Grand Total for 20th AF 414 combat losses
104 non-combat losses
Another 10 B-29s were lost en route from the USA to combat theaters.
Altogether 528 B-29s were lost, April 1944–August 1945

Below: **P2B-IS (background), used as a launch platform for the Bell X-1A Skyrocket.**

5. Aircraft Strength of 20th Air Force April 1944–August 1945

(Figures include first and second line aircraft)

Year and Month	Aircraft available	Crews available
April 1944	94	143
May	137	222
June	133	226
July	146	224
August	150	221
September	163	221
October	219	287
November	262	391
December	348	484
January 1945	450	579
February	541	688
March	605	778
April	708	870
May	732	880
June	888	1106
July	998	1186
August	1056	1378

6. Bomb Tonnage Dropped by 20th Air Force on Japan June 1944–August 1945

(Atomic bombs not included)

A. XX Bomber Command

Year and Month	High Explosive	Incendiary
June 1944	501	46
July	209	—
August	184	68
September	521	—
October	1023	646
November	1415	215
December	1556	—
January 1945	1584	422
February	1261	604
March	1019	417
	9273	2418

B. XXI Bomber Command

Year and Month	High Explosive	Incendiary
November 1944	343	232
December	1,495	610
January 1945	927	477
February	1,140	1,015
March	3,086	10,761
April	13,209	4,283
May	6,937	17,348
June	9,954	22,588
July	9,388	33,163
August	8,438	12,591
	54,917	103,068

Grand Totals 20th AF dropped   64,190 tons HE
105,486 tons Incendiaries
on Japan between June 1944 and August 1945

7. B-29s in the Korean War, 1950–53

Units involved

19th Bomb Group of
20th Air Force — operative throughout the campaign.
22nd Bomb Wing of SAC } transferred to FEAF 3 July and
92nd Bomb Wing of SAC } returned to USA 27 October 1950
98th Bomb Wing of SAC } transferred to FEAF 30 July 1950, and
307th Bomb Wing of SAC } returned to USA July 1953
31st Strategic Reconnaissance Squadron of SAC } (renamed 91st SRS on 16 November 1950) operative throughout the campaign using RB-29s

(The terms Bomb Group and Bomb Wing do not appear to have meant the same in 1950 as they did in 1945. Regardless of the nomenclature, each consisted of two squadrons only, so it would seem that whereas 20th AF had maintained the organization, albeit on a reduced scale, of World War II, SAC had taken the Bomb Wing as its basic unit, again on a reduced scale, when formed in 1947. In any event the existence of the two names has caused confusion among writers on the B-29)

Statistics

Aircraft sorties flown	21,000
Tons of bombs dropped	167,000
B-29s lost	34 (16 to enemy fighters 4 to enemy anti-aircraft defenses 14 to other causes, including accident)

Markings

Basic markings were as they had been during World War II, with the addition of the words 'United States Air Force' on both sides of the forward upper fuselage and the letters 'USAF' above the starboard and below the port mainplanes. SAC aircraft carried the SAC crest on the tail fin

Fin markings were the same as the later revisions of the Marianas operations – a letter within a geometric shape. So the 22nd BW carried 'W' within a circle, the 98th BW an 'H' within a square; 31st (91st) SRS an 'X' within a circle

Bibliography

B-29 Superfortress at War, David A Anderton, Ian Allan, 1978

B-29: The Superfortress, Carl Berger, Ballantine Books, 1970

Boeing Aircraft since 1916, Peter M Bowers, Putnam and Company, 1966

The Army Air Forces in World War II, Kit C Carter and Robert Mueller, Combat Chronology, 1941–45 Government Printing Office, Washington, 1975

The Army Air Forces in World War II, Volume Five: 'The Pacific: Matterhorn to Nagasaki', Wesley F Craven and James L Cate, University of Chicago Press, 1953

The US Strategic Bomber, Roger Freeman, Macdonald and Jane's, 1975

Combat Aircraft of World War II, Bill Gunston, Salamander Books, 1978

Air War over Korea, Robert Jackson, Ian Allan, 1975

Ruin from the Air, Gordon Thomas and Max M Witts, Sphere Books, 1978

Acknowledgments

The author would like to thank the Taylor Picture Library, Robert Hunt and Carina Dvorak for supplying the pictures for this book. The publisher would like to thank the following picture libraries and individuals for the following pictures:

Boeing Aircraft Company: pp 10, 11, 12–13, 14, 15 (center), 19 (bottom), 23 (top left), 23 (bottom), 27 (center), 28–29, 29 (bottom right), 52 (top right), 57.
Imperial War Museum: pp 6–7 (bottom four), 22 (bottom right).
National Archives: pp 8, 26–27.
Robert Hunt Library: pp 9 (top), 27 (top right), 34 (top).

Bob Snyder: p 7 (top).
Taylor Picture Library: pp 2–3, 4–5, 6–7 (main picture), 15 (top), 16, 20–21, 24–25, 36 (bottom), 59.
USAF: pp 1, 9 (bottom), 19 (top), 26 (bottom), 29 (bottom left), 31 (bottom), 32–33, 34 (bottom), 35, 36 (top), 37, 38, 39, 40–41, 42–43, 44, 45, 46, 47, 48, 49, 50, 52 (top left), 52–53 (bottom), 54, 55, 56, 64.

US Army: pp 27 (top left), 31 (top), 51
US Navy: p 23 (top).

Artwork

Mike Badrocke: Cutaway on pp 12–13, line drawings on p 59.
Mike Bailey: Cover sideview.
Mike Trim: Sideview on pp 14–15.

Below: **SB-29 'Superdumbo' rescue aircraft, with lifeboat slung beneath forward fuselage.**